M & A for
Value Creation in Japan

Monden Institute of Management: Japanese Management and International Studies (ISSN: 1793-2874)

Editor-in-Chief: Yasuhiro Monden *(Mejiro University, Japan)*

Published

Vol. 1   Value-Based Management of the Rising Sun
edited by Yasuhiro Monden, Kanji Miyamoto, Kazuki Hamada, Gunyung Lee & Takayuki Asada

Vol. 2   Japanese Management Accounting Today
edited by Yasuhiro Monden, Masanobu Kosuga, Yoshiyuki Nagasaka, Shufuku Hiraoka & Noriko Hoshi

Vol. 3   Japanese Project Management:
KPM — Innovation, Development and Improvement
edited by Shigenobu Ohara & Takayuki Asada

Vol. 4   International Management Accounting in Japan:
Current Status of Electronics Companies
edited by Kanji Miyamoto

Vol. 5   Business Process Management of Japanese and Korean Companies
edited by Gunyung Lee, Masanobu Kosuga, Yoshiyuki Nagasaka & Byungkyu Sohn

Vol. 6   M&A for Value Creation in Japan
edited by Yasuyoshi Kurokawa

Forthcoming

Business Group Management in Japan
edited by Kazuki Hamada

Monden Institute of Management
Japanese Management and International Studies – Vol. 6

M & A for
Value Creation in Japan

Yasuyoshi Kurokawa
Senshu University, Japan

 **World Scientific**

NEW JERSEY · LONDON · SINGAPORE · BEIJING · SHANGHAI · HONG KONG · TAIPEI · CHENNAI

Published by

World Scientific Publishing Co. Pte. Ltd.

5 Toh Tuck Link, Singapore 596224

USA office: 27 Warren Street, Suite 401-402, Hackensack, NJ 07601

UK office: 57 Shelton Street, Covent Garden, London WC2H 9HE

Library of Congress Cataloging-in-Publication Data
M&A for value creation in Japan / edited by Yasuyoshi Kurokawa.
    p. cm. -- (Monden Institute of Management: Japanese management and international studies,
1793-2874 ; v. 6)
    Includes bibliographical references and index.
    ISBN-13: 978-9814287463 (alk. paper)
    ISBN-10: 9814287466 (alk. paper)
    1. Consolidation and merger of corporations--Japan. 2. Corporations--Valuation--Japan.
I. Kurokawa, Yasuyoshi. II. Monden Institute of Management and Accounting.
III. Title: M and A for value creation in Japan. IV. Title: M & A for value creation in Japan.
    HD2746.55.J3M2195 2010
    658.1'620952--dc22
                                                                                    2009042571

British Library Cataloguing-in-Publication Data
A catalogue record for this book is available from the British Library.

Typeset by Stallion Press
Email: enquiries@stallionpress.com

Printed in Singapore.

Japan Society of Organization and Accounting

Mission of JSOA and Editorial Information

For the purpose of making a contribution to the business and academic communities, the Japan Society of Organization and Accounting (JSOA), a reformed and expanded organization from the Monden Institute of Management, is committed to publishing the book series, entitled *Japanese Management and International Studies*, with a refereed system.

Focusing on Japan and Japan-related issues, the series is designed to inform the world about research outcomes of the new "Japanese-style management system" developed in Japan. It includes the Japanese version of management systems developed abroad. In addition, it publishes research by foreign scholars and concerning foreign systems that constitute significant points of comparison with the Japanese system.

Research topics included in this series are management of organizations in a broad sense (including the business group) and the accounting that supports the organization. More specifically, topics include business strategy, organizational restructuring, corporate finance, M&A, environmental management, business models, operations management, managerial accounting, financial accounting for organizational restructuring, manager performance evaluation, remuneration systems, and management of revenues and costs. The research approach is interdisciplinary, which includes case studies, theoretical studies, normative studies and empirical studies, but emphasizes real world business.

Each volume contains the series title and a book title which reflects the volume's special theme.

Our JSOA's board of directors has established an editorial board of international standing, which is served by the Monden Institute of Management. In each volume, guest editors who are experts on the volume's special theme serve as the volume editors.

Editorial Board

Contents

List of Contributors

Yasuyoshi Kurokawa
Professor, Faculty of Commerce, Senshu University
2-1-1, Higashimita, Tamaku, Kawasaki-shi
Kanagawa 214-8580, Japan
Email: kurokawa@isc.senshu-u.ac.jp

Yujiro Okura
Professor, Faculty of Commerce, Kansai University
3-3-35 Yamate-cho, Suita-shi, Osaka 564-8680, Japan
Email: yokura@ipcku.kansai-u.ac.jp

Kunimaru Takahashi
Professor, Faculty of Business Administration
Aoyama Gakuin University
4-4-25, Shibuya, Shibuya-ku, Tokyo 150-8366, Japan
Email: kuni@busi.aoyama.ac.jp

Michio Kunimura
Professor, Department of Business and Management
Meijo University, 1-501, Shiokamakuchi
Tenpaku-ku, Nagoya-shi, Nagoya 468-8502, Japan
Email: kunimura@ccmfs.meijo-u.ac.jp

Yasuhiro Monden
Professor, Faculty of Business Administration, Mejiro University
4-31-1 Nakaochiai, Shinjyuku-ku, Tokyo 161-8539, Japan
Email: monden@mejiro.ac.jp

Tatsushi Yamamoto
Professor, Graduate School of Economics of Economics
Nagoya University, Furoucho, Chikusa-ku
Nagoya 464-8601, Japan
Email: yamamoto@soec.nagoya-u.ac.jp

Keiichi Sugiura
Representative Director
Japan Buy-out Research Institute Corporation
30th Floor, Pacific Century Place Marunouchi
11-1, Marunouchi 1-chome, Chiyoda-ku, Tokyo, 100-6230, Japan
Email: bm980115@toyonet.toyo.ac.jp

Kotaro Inoue
Associate Professor
Graduate School of Business Administration, Keio University
4-1-1, Hiyoshi, Kouhoku-ku, Yokohama-shi
Kanagawa, 223-8521, Japan
Email: kotaro.i@hc.cc.keio.ac.jp

1

Accounting Problems Encountered in M&As

Yasuyoshi Kurokawa

Professor, Faculty of Commerce, Senshu University

1 Introduction

In recent years, with the sudden spread of globalization and the rapid accumulation of business information, companies are forced to cope with a growing number of emergency situations. Accounting standards for business combinations in Japan have been announced in the "Opinion on the Establishment of Accounting Standards for Business Combinations" issued by the Business Accounting Deliberation Council in October, 2003. The "Accounting Standards for Business Combinations" based on this opinion have been applied from the accounting period beginning on April 1, 2006.

This opinion is based on the idea of government fostering of enterprises with international competitive power. It proposes the reorganization of international enterprises in particular. In addition, it encourages the harmonization of Japanese accounting standards with international accounting standards. By international accounting standards, this paper refers to the International Financial Reporting Standard (IFRS) published by the International Accounting Standards Board (IASB) and the Statement of Financial Accounting Standards (SFAS) published by the Financial Accounting Standards Board (FASB). By approximating these international standards, it is expected that the capital market of our country will be reactivated and that the globalization of enterprises will progress.

The activation of the capital market is not achieved only through examination of M&As; however, it is achieved by joining M&A

accounting with corporate governance. Taking into consideration the interests of all stakeholders simultaneously, we will clarify the process of globalization of the capital market in Japan and the ideal method of governance through an examination of M&A accounting.

2 The Present Conditions of M&A Accounting in Japan: Stepping toward International Harmonization

The Financial Accounting Standards Board (FASB) in the States did not adopt the *pooling of interests* method, but the *purchase* method for business combination in its Statement of Financial Reporting Standards No. 141, "Business Combinations," issued in June 2001. And in the case of a merger of equals, the FASB examined the possibility of adopting the *fresh start* method, because it is unknown which is the acquiring company (SFAS No. 141, paragraph B32) (Kikuya, 2007, p. 18). However, the IASB published IFRS No. 3 to force the purchase method through in March 2004; this statement is an example of the American disregard of the fresh start method.

The Japanese Accounting Standards for Business Combinations have recognized the pooling of interests method, while assuming the purchase method basics. Because we cannot distinguish the acquiring company from the acquired one, the pooling of interests method is used in order to circumvent the limitations inherent in commercial law. According to commercial law, we cannot replace a continuing company with a company legally becoming extinct. It follows that the pooling of interests method did not disappear as a means to absorb the value of the company which continues. In adopting the purchase method, the standard of our country basically follows the same path as the international trend. However, the Japanese standard is slightly different from the international one in its application of the purchase method.

The Japanese Accounting Standards for Business Combinations gives control to both the controlling company and the controlled company in the same way. The rule does not have to make it clear which is the controlling company. However, even if the purchase method is adopted for this reason, the pooling of interests method is also accepted. The IFRS adopts the purchase method with the highest precedence from the viewpoint that either company is in control. In this sense, SFS No. 141 and IFRS hold the same stance.

When we define acquisition in our country, we ordinarily mean anything other than a situation satisfying all of the three matters listed below (Accounting Standards Board of Japan (ASBJ), Accounting Standards for Business Combinations III-1- (1), 2004):

1. The counter value is represented by stocks with voting right.
2. The voting rights are equal.
3. The condition that the acquisition reflects all controlling relations except the voting right ratio is not satisfied.

But, only when the points 1 and 3 in the above list are satisfied, the resulting merger is treated as a synarchy company and it becomes a combination of the participating equities (ASBJ, Accounting Standards for Business Combinations III-1- (2), 2004).

When a business combination occurs in which there is counter value other than stocks with voting right, the company that expends counter value becomes the acquiring company, and when the counter value consists of stocks with voting right, the company that has the larger voting right ratio becomes the acquiring company. When the voting right ratio is equal, the matter is judged based on control-related facts. The control-related facts are recognized to imply control if, among the following four conditions, even one holds:

1. Constituting the majority of members of the decision-making body.
2. Having the decision-making right with regard to financial affairs and management policies.
3. Getting rid of most of the business within two years.
4. The exchange ratio of stocks to be issued for the counter value is estranged with the exchange ratio calculated based on the current price, and a large premium is paid.

The IFRS defines the acquiring entity as "the company with dominance." It is assumed that the dominance consists of having various types of authority (IFRS, paragraphs 17–19). As for authority, the following characteristics are assumed (ASBJ, Accounting Standards for Business Combinations "2 of accounting standards" III-1- (2), 2004):

1. The majority of the voting right is held.
2. The decision-making right with regard to financial affairs and management policies is held.
3. The majority of the voting right of the majority of the governing bodies is held.
4. The majority of the voting right of the governing bodies is held (ASBJ, Accounting Standards for Business Combinations, Explanatory Notes, Note 4, 2004).

However, when identifying the dominant company, this issue is sometimes unclear at the time of M&A. Therefore, the IFRS defines dominance, i.e., the acquiring entity, based on the following three criteria:

1. When the fair market value of a certain company is remarkably larger than the fair value of the other company, it is obvious that the larger company is the acquiring entity.
2. When M&A is carried out by means of cash or other assets in exchange for the voting right common stock, it is obvious that the company that hands over the cash or other assets is the acquiring entity.
3. It is obvious that the company whose manager becomes the manager of the company resulting from the M&A is the acquiring entity.

The aim of the IFRS is to make it clear which is the controlling company, as discussed above, and to discourage the unification of interests into a synarchy as a result of not correctly identifying the controlling company.

The FASB regards the company which hands over assets for the counter value or takes over the debt as the acquiring entity (FASB, 2001, SFS No. 141, paragraph 16). However, in the case of a stock swap, the company publishing stocks may not be the controlling company, because a controlled company can also publish stocks. The controlling company is distinguished by the situation of the voting right after the combination, the governing bodies, the administration structure, and the bargaining points of the equity security (FASB, 2001, SFS No. 141, paragraph 17).

The accounting standards of the IFRS and SFS focus on the identification of the acquiring entity. In contrast, the Japanese accounting standards consider both sides, i.e., the acquiring entity as well as the acquired one.

The next problem when the controlling company becomes an acquiring entity is how it calculates the cost the acquired entity. The acquiring entity assumes as the historical cost the total amount of money corresponding to the fair value of the assets and liabilities of the acquired entity and the accompanying additional expenses at the time of acquisition. In this regard, SFS No. 141, IFRS No. 3 and the Japanese Accounting Standards for Business Combinations are similar.

However, the calculation of the historical cost when the acquiring entity publishes the equity securities held in the acquired entity is slightly different in SFS No. 141, IFRS No. 3, and the Japanese standards.

IFRS No. 3 takes the price as of the day of exchange of the securities (acquisition date model) (paragraph 27). However, in Japan, this situation is handled as an exception. In other words, the acquisition date model takes the price on the acquisition day when the stock prices on the stock swap day are not widely different from the stock prices before the agreement/publication date of the main condition of the M&A. In principle, the Japanese accounting standards adopt the agreement date model, in that the main conditions of the M&A are agreed upon and the stock prices announced several days prior are taken as valid (ASBJ, Accounting Standards for Business Combinations III-2- (2), (3), 2004).

SFS No. 141 clarifies the main condition: the stock prices that are announced within a reasonable period before and after are taken as valid; however, the stock prices announced several days prior are not valid. On this point, there is a slight difference between the SFS and the Japanese standards; however, the agreement day model is straightforward and easily applied (Kikuya, 2007, p. 25).

The acquiring entity recognizes the identifiable assets and liabilities of the acquired entity at their fair market value on the acquisition day and makes the cost allocation after the business combination according to the respective assets and liabilities for the year ahead. When the legal right and the transferable intangible assets are included in the acquired assets, the relevant intangible assets can be allocated by the cost. The timing of the recognition of the liabilities is as follows. The expense or loss for which accrual is predicted in the short term after the acquisition, as well as the possibility of accrual, is reflected in the calculation of the acquisition price. In this way, the Japanese standard isolates the cost allocation of the acquired entity over the one-year period after the acquisition and it recognizes the fair value of the assets and liabilities on the acquisition day. However, evaluation of concrete and the identifiable assets and liabilities is necessary for the determination of the fair value of the acquired entity. Regarding assets and liabilities, it will be necessary to apply the replacement cost, the estimated amounts that subtracted the amount of profit equivalency, the sale expense from the market value, the present discount value, and the selling price as per IFRS No. 3 and SFS No. 141.

The Accounting Standards Board of Japan, which has taken over the work of the Business Accounting Deliberation Council, revises the accounting standards for M&As, and the next standard will become valid in April 2010. The revised standards will consist of the following:

1. Corporate Accounting Standard No. 21, Accounting Standards for Business Combinations.
2. Corporate Accounting Standard No. 22, Accounting Standards for Consolidated Financial Statements.
3. Corporate Accounting Standard No. 23, partial revision of the Accounting Standards for Research and Development Expenses.
4. Revision of Corporate Accounting Standard No. 7, Accounting Standards for Business Separations.
5. Revision of Corporate Accounting Standard No. 16, Accounting Standards for the Equity Method.

6. Revision of the Guideline for the Application of Corporate Accounting Standard No. 10, Guideline for the Application of the Accounting Standards for Business Combinations and Accounting Standards for Business Separations.

The most important characteristic of the new standard is that it abolishes the pooling of interests method, in which the acquiring entity takes over the assets and debts of the acquired entity at their book value. When the purchase method is adopted, goodwill is generated. That is to say, on the side of the acquiring entity, when the historical cost is unequal to the sum of the assets of the acquired entity and the liabilities undertaken, the surplus is entered in the assets column as *goodwill* and the deficiency is entered in the liabilities column as *negative goodwill*.

Until now, depending on the actual situation of the acquisition, the negative goodwill was written off regularly over a period of 20 years and entered as non-operating profit. However, with the new standard, it will be entered as an *extraordinary gain* in the year when it is purchased. In other words, the negative goodwill is extinguished by applying the *immediate reversal* method.

In addition, the acquiring company used to treat [what] as an expense at the time of cost allocation; we used to treat a part of the historical cost, including the cost of software, as research and development expenses. However, it was treated as an asset if a certain condition was satisfied, and expense processing came to be widely accepted.

When the acquiring company issued stocks in exchange for the value of the acquisition, the current price of the property was based on the stock prices before the day when the main condition was agreed upon and the combination was announced.

However, the new Japanese accounting standards acknowledge the current cost on the day of the M&A or the day of separation of a business. In other words, when stocks are issued for the value of the acquisition, the standard of our country will change from the agreement day model stipulated in SFS No. 141 to the acquisition day model expressed in IFRS No. 3.

Positive goodwill is appropriated together with the assets and it is amortized regularly over a period of 20 years by the method of fixed installment and others. The amortization of goodwill is included in the selling expenses and administrative expenses, but it cannot be put down to special losses except in the case of impairment loss. When the amount acquired goodwill is negligible, it can be treated as an expense and displayed as a selling expense or administrative expense. The non-amortized balance of goodwill becomes the object of impairment treatment and, in this case, there must be a sign of the impairment in the M&A year.

Regarding the sign, there are cases in which the amount of money allocated to intangible assets other than goodwill is large, and a large premium is paid. When impairment loss of goodwill is recognized, it is entered in the special losses section.

According to the new standard, positive goodwill will be amortized regularly and impairment accounting is limited when a sign of the impairment is seen in the M&A year. This is different from the international trend reflected in International Financial Reporting Standard No. 3 (IFRS3) of the IASB and Financial Accounting Standard No. 14 (SFAS14) of the AFASB. In other words, the assets which are appropriated as assets are measured as the amount of money resulting from the subtraction of the total impairment loss. The assets are not amortized regularly, but an impairment test must be conducted every year.

Therefore, the IASB and FASB require that regular amortization be subtracted from the assets which are appropriated as assets, and that only the impairment test method be adopted (Kikuya, 2007, p. 25).

In addition, when preparing the consolidated financial statement, the *purchased goodwill* method, namely the *partial current cost* method, which reflects only the minority interests in the evaluation of the assets and liabilities of the subsidiary, will be abandoned. Instead, the *full goodwill* method will be introduced in the new standard. This method is also called the *"full current cost evaluation"* method and it evaluates the assets and liabilities of all subsidiaries at the current cost on the acquisition day (Consolidated Accounting Standards of Japan, Article 20).

In other words, the fair value of the subsidiary is established for all assets of the subsidiary; not only for the identifiable assets and liabilities but also for the unidentifiable ones. Goodwill is also included in the fair value evaluation of a non-controlling shareholder's equity. It is said that this accounting treatment harmonizes with the economic unit concept. Goodwill recognized based on identifiable assets is distributed proportionally over the non-controlling shareholder's equity and, even if not all the equity is acquired, all of it is evaluated based on the fair market value, including the non-controlling shareholder's equity. The reason for this is that there is no difference between the way of handling the parent company's equity and that of handling the minority interests. Adding the internally generated goodwill accompanying the non-controlling shareholder's equity and the reliability of goodwill measurement in the full goodwill method is pointed out as problematic (Kikuya, 2007, p. 28).

3 The Revision of the Accounting Standards for Business Combinations: Toward Convergence

The M&A accounting standards of our country, in which the pooling of interests method is abolished and the purchase method is introduced, face the problem of whether have only to say that the globalization of merely accounting standards is submitted.

The following is often given as grounds for adopting the pooling of interests method. After a business combination, the equities of the parties simply continue to exist in the same mutual ratio and the settlement of investment and reinvestment is not to be it. However, one reason for supporting the purchase method is that this method lacks validity because it allows for a change in quality of the equity. But the change in quality of the equity is accepted by both sides, and in pooling the interests, it is argued against the adoption of the purchase method (Mandai, 2003a).

This is relevant in investment decision making, because the pooling of interests method, which recognizes assets and liabilities at book value and ignores predicted cash flow, lacks purpose adaptability. It is thought that the investment decision-making utility lacks relevance. Even if the cash flow in the future will reflect the fair value of the assets and liabilities and the purchase method discloses the absolute amount of the share, the cash flow in the future cannot be known today, because it is not the absolute sum of the share, but is calculated based on the profit realized in the future. The corporate value is calculated by discounting future profit and future cash flow from the realized profit. Therefore, there is no ground for adopting the purchase method (Mandai, 2003b).

In addition, there are dissenting opinions regarding the fact that goodwill is not amortized or handled as impairment. There is no objection to the idea that unidentifiable assets bring future economic benefit in the form of goodwill. However, the following three issues are examined when determining whether goodwill should be amortized or handled as impairment or not.

1. The combination of regular amortization and impairment.
2. Non-amortization and impairment.
3. The combination of points 1 and 2, (i.e., regular amortization and impairment and non-amortization and impairment).

Of these, point 3 will be rejected from the standpoint of the comparability of financial statements. As for point 1, regular amortization is objected to because it is only an arbitrary estimate, which makes it uncertain whether the amortization cost of the goodwill is economical or not. However, there is no reason to reject the regular amortization of goodwill even if regular amortization is an arbitrary estimate. In addition, the amortization cost of goodwill is economical, as long as we recognize that the value of goodwill in itself, as excess earning power, decreases slowly.

If a strict and feasible impairment test is possible, it becomes a useful processing method. It is not feasible to test often when we see a sign of the impairment.

Even if this impairment test takes the book value of the goodwill and compares it with the presumed price, it is not a strict and feasible impairment test, because internally created goodwill may enter the tested data (Mandai, 2003b). We must recognize internally created goodwill if we are going to adopt the point 2 given above. It may be said that it is not a stage to recognize internally created goodwill, as long as we choose point 1, the combination of regular amortization and impairment, and not point 2 in the new standard.

3.1 M&A accounting standards (established in 2003, enforced in 2006)

1. The classification ∼ acquisition
   ∼ Unification of interests
2. Accounting method ∼ acquisition ∼ purchase method
   Unification of interests ∼ pooling of interests method
3. Goodwill ∼ regular amortization over a period of 20 years
   (or immediate amortization)
4. Negative goodwill ∼ regular reversal over a period of 20 years
   (or immediate reversal)

3.2 Revised M&A accounting standards (established in 2009, will be enforced in 2010)

1. The classification ∼ acquisition
2. Accounting method ∼ acquisition ∼ purchase method
3. Goodwill ∼ regular amortization over a period of 20 years
   The amortized balance becomes the object of impairment (extraordinary loss)
4. Negative goodwill ∼ profit within the accounting period (extraordinary gain)

The Japanese accounting system was completed with the adoption of the purchase method, as a result of choosing between the purchase method and the pooling of interests method. As an extension of this choice, the fresh start method may be argued for in the future. This was the reason for the revision of commercial law in acknowledgment of the use of the transfer of stocks system.

Transfer of stocks where "a fully joint company is established by all the parent companies" is performed by corporate groups encompassing many types of industry. The IASB introduced the fresh start method into M&A accounting for cases where a joint venture is established as a deliberation matter for the future of project summary in April 2002 (Daigo, 2003, p. 143).

In the transfer of stocks where "a fully joint company is established by all the parent companies," the founding parent company has difficulty adopting the purchase method since the company does not become the acquiring entity.

However, in this case, the fresh start method reflects the actual economic situation of the birth of a new company. In other words, the founding parent company is not the acquiring entity; instead, a new company is formed by the transfer of stocks in a process resembling a joint venture, and the target company is the company targeted before the combination. If we think in this way, the fresh start method is reasonable.

Because the new company is recognized as a unified entity, the accounting treatment of the goodwill must be reexamined. The problem is how to understand the *synergy goodwill* reflected in the transfer of stocks of "the fully joint company established by all the parent companies" (Daigo, 2003, p. 151).

Synergy goodwill is characterized by the following two traits:

1. The fair value of the going concern element of the target company. It derives from the synergy of the target company's business.
2. Both the prospective net assets generated from the combination of the acquiring entity and the acquired entity and the synergy fairness value of the business.

Point 1 in the above list represents goodwill already present at the time of combination, while point 2 is prospective goodwill generated by the business fusion; these two are collectively called "core goodwill." The core goodwill is generated by the business fusion. Therefore, the birth of core goodwill will be interpreted as the birth of a new company, as long as the business combination produces a synergy effect and it raises the corporate value. This becomes the ground for adopting the fresh start method for the transfer of stocks where "a fully joint company is established by all the parent companies"(Daigo, 2003, pp. 143–155).

4 Reexamination of Governance Based on Stockholder Dominance

M&As are on the increase in our country, but there is no particular increase in the number of remarkable M&As, the important thing to note; however, there is no tendency of decrease that has been seen recently. With the increase of M&As, the manager of the target enterprise and its employees sustain great economic impact. Although this point has been understood to some extent, it remains difficult to grasp the degree of influence exerted by all the shareholders together on the acquiring entity and the acquired entity. Controversy rages over whether shareholder value increases or decreases and whether that value is protected or not.

Because it is thought that a manager tends to infringe on shareholder value, the prevailing opinion is that the manager needs monitoring. This role has been fulfilled by an outside monitoring agency, such as a bank, a *keiretsu*, a chief shareholder, a pension fund, or a person who can carry out a hostile buyout. This problem belongs to the economy of M&As.

However, some believe that the shareholder value does not rise if neither the outside monitoring nor the internal monitoring functions. Internal monitoring is a duty fulfilled by the board of directors (Watanabe, Inoue, and Sayama, 2007, pp. 5–9). It is very likely to contribute to the raising of the shareholder value, even if internal monitoring becomes an obligatory task of the board of directors. However, it is also necessary to monitor the stockholders as a group when stewarding the shareholder value.

As a starting point in grasping the issue of corporate governance through accounting, Professor Aishi Imafuku does not regard it as a problem of contracts with the stockholders based on conventional agency, but thinks of the manager of a company as a "fiduciary" officer (Imafuku, 2003, pp. 3–4). Here, the idea that the manager represents and substitutes for the stockholder is abandoned. The reason is that the manager is not concerned with handling contract relations with the stockholders; rather, his main objective is to raise the corporate value of the assets entrusted to him. Today, this viewpoint is becoming generalized.

The following four problems are relevant when wielding corporate governance through accounting (Imafuku, 2003, p. 5):

1. Accounting in corporate governance is premised on the investors, not the stockholder public.
2. Accounting in corporate governance focuses on the quality of the financial reports, not the validity of the accounting method used to prepare financial reports.
3. The main task of accounting in corporate governance is to make calculations based on the accounting information of the company; the preparation of financial reports is secondary.
4. The study of accounting in corporate governance has its object; the establishment and the establishment mechanism of accounting standards enable the creation of autonomous accounting information within the company.

Regarding the points mentioned above, let us add the following explanations. Point 1 does not refer to a simple investor. The contemporary investor has confidence in the manager's stewardship of funds. Point 2 means that, from the viewpoint of accounting culture, the financial reporting system encourages the reexamination of the quality of positive accounting and conservative accounting. In point 3, the separation of the decision making team from the executive team of the company must be reflected in the organizational structure and the calculation process of the accounting information must be taken into consideration. In brief, point 4 suggests the unification of the organizations that establish accounting standards, in order to unify the accounting model systems reflected in points 1, 2, and 3.

The manager is trusted by the stockholders to make the best use of the company's assets, as well as to raise the corporate value. In this case, in accounting, the corporate value is identified with the total company's assets, and the total assets consist of the total net assets and total liabilities. If we monitor the corporate value based on market evaluation, it is estimated as the current price of the stocks and the market valuation of the liability. However, the corporate value when performing M&As is estimated as the grand total of the asking price of the buyer and the transfer liability (Aomatsu, 2008, pp. 29–30). Thus, corporate value can be evaluated in various ways. A corporate value grasped to being common as a base is expectation cash flow namely cash flow brought from an existing business and a future growth opportunity than the past and present cash flow (Hachiya, 2004, p. 154).

In investor relations, investors do not object to taking corporate social responsibility (CSR) as long as the corporate value is controlled by the investors. Therefore, in order to substantially improve the corporate value, a manager must recognize the importance of cash flow management and CSR.

CSR must be central to the activity of a company and it must consider all the stakeholders. If I can call this stakeholder profit, it is necessary to make a clear difference between corporate value, shareholder value, and stakeholder profit. Shareholder value is at the core of this trio; further out lies corporate value and furthest lies stakeholder profit. Shareholder value is central because the company does not exist without the financing provided by the stockholders. In a company that avails itself of financing, corporate activity that considers not only shareholder value but also stakeholder profit becomes essential for the improvement of the corporate value (Aomatsu, pp. 23–26).

5 Conclusion

The accelerating wave of M&As is spreading throughout the world. We are insufficient only by knowing the market or the industry for the complexity whether you lead this to the success. The practical application of highly complicated technical knowledge has become crucial. And technical knowledge must not be employed piecemeal: the most important way to ensure success is to use comprehensive and interdisciplinary knowledge.

However, this comprehensive perspective must also encompass corporate governance, because the practice of M&As should attach great importance to the requirements of not only financial allocation but also of the various parties involved.

Corporate value is changing into a pluralistic phenomenon involving various categories of stakeholders; it is no longer centered exclusively on stockholders. By stakeholders, we mean not only creditors and stockholders, but also suppliers, consumers, employees, the community, and stakeholders in the environment. Corporate governance changes with the expansion of the concept of stakeholder. Today, the ideal method of corporate governance takes into consideration capitalist as well as non-capitalist goals and is inherently multi-dimensional. Social value and environmental value are included in the range of corporate purposes, which means what corporate value must be evaluated from a multi-dimensional perspective.

References

Aomatsu, H (2008). *Corporate Value Lecture*, Nihon Keizai Shimbun Pub. Co. (in Japanese).

Daigo, S (2003). Accounting standards for business combinations and an application for transfer of equity interests. In *Accounting for Reorganization*, Daigo, S (ed.), Tokyo Keizai Jyouhou Pub. Co. (in Japanese).

Hachiya, T (2004). Cash flow-evaluation of value of enterprise by information. In *Cash Flow Accounting and Valuation of Enterprise*, Ito, K (ed.), Chuoukeizasha (in Japanese).

Imafuku, A (2003). Accounting and corporate governance. *Accounting*, 163(4) (in Japanese).

Kikuya, M (2007). International convergence of business combination accounting standards. *Keieisirin*, 43(4), 17–30 (in Japanese).

Mandai, K (2003a). Accounting for business combination – logic of the purchase method unification in IFRS, *Corporate Accounting*, 55(7), 68–69 (in Japanese).

Mandai, K (2003b). Accounting for business combination – logic of the non amortization in goodwill. *Corporate Accounting*, 55(8), 84–85 (in Japanese).

Watanabe, A, K Inoue and N Sayama (2007). *M&A and Governance*, Chuou Keizasha (in Japanese).

2

A Study of Goodwill and Intangible Fixed Asset on Business Combination: Pharmaceutical Companies in Japan

Yujiro Okura

Professor of Accounting, Kansai University in Japan

The relationship between the parent company and the wholly owned subsidiary was established by Daiichi Pharmaceutical Co., Ltd. and Sankyo Company Limited exchanging stocks with Daiichi Sankyo Company Limited in September, 2005. Daiichi Sankyo Company Limited was obliged to submit Form 4 to the Securities and Exchange Commission (SEC) in June 2005, because the percentage of foreign shareholders of Daiichi Sankyo Company Limited was 32.7%. The purpose of this paper is to examine whether or not the evaluation was reasonable in deciding this share transfer percentage in accounting for goodwill and evaluation of intangible assets from study development. This examination is the first step in establishing the evaluation method in this field.

1 Prior Studies Concerning the Reasonability of the Adoption of the Free Cash Flow Method

I will first examine prior studies on the relationship between the DCF method (discounted free cash flow) adopted in the share transfer ratio and the share prices. There are two prior studies; an empirical analysis by Richard G. Sloan[1] and a theoretical study by John R. Mills and Jeanne H. Yamamura. I take up the former here. The results relating to this paper out of the study by Richard G. Sloan (samples of 40,679 companies for the period from 1962 to 1991) are as follows.

First, regression analysis of estimated future earnings ($t+1$ period "earnings $t + 1 = r0 + r1$ accruals $t + r1$ cashflows $t + Vt + 1$." Here, earnings means earnings from continuous business for the current term/average total assets, and accruals means (non-cash liquid assets − (short-term borrowings and liquid liabilities excluding tax paid) – depreciation/average total assets), and that is working capital. Operating cash flow is the difference between these earnings and the accruals.

According to this result, the effect on estimated future earnings ($t+1$ period) is that operating cash flow is greater than accrual working capital (working capital). In this case, the coefficient of operating cash flow (t period), which is 0.855, is greater than the coefficient of accrual component elements (t period), which is 0.765.

Second, earning results by extreme working capital will return to the original state at the end of the third year and earning results by extreme operating cash flow will return to the original state at the end of the second year.

Third, the component ratio of accruals to earnings depends on the size of liquid assets, especially on the notes and accounts receivable and inventories, and changes without a relationship with notes and accounts payable.

Fourth, because investors tend to stick to reported earnings, abnormal share price earnings can be obtained by wrongly using the inability of investors to differentiate accrual component elements from cash flow component elements in earnings. In particular, long positions of companies that report a relatively low level of accruals to the level of cash flows and short positions of companies that report a relatively high level of accruals to the level of cash flows generate abnormal share price earnings.

2 Corporate Evaluation of Business Combination Accounting and PPA

The evaluation of corporate value for the purpose of corporate reorganization will be carried out by the unit of a corporate group, which is shown below.

First, evaluation of corporate value is evaluation of total investment amount; in other words, the total amount of consideration paid. The ratio of share transfer is made to seek the net asset value per share, which is not only in net asset value but also in business value including goodwill and intangible and intellectual assets that show excess earning power, which will be deducted from borrowed capital such as interest bearing liabilities. The center of the income approach is therefore cash flow.

Second, purchase price application (PPA) in evaluation of transfer assets and liabilities in the purchase method is made as provision of information that fairly reflects a transaction of a merger, in financial statements within a year after a business combination. Identifiable individual assets and liabilities are evaluated on the basis of market value and fairly distributed into respective items. Here, revaluation is made not only in financial assets and tangible assets but also in intangible assets.

Third, where a difference arises between evaluation of total investment amount, that is to say, total amount of consideration paid and net amount distributed to under individual assets and liabilities at market value, the excess amount will be recognized as goodwill or a negative goodwill. Typical goodwill is excess earnings power by sales synergy as pressures on sales channels, cost synergy by factory intensification, reduction of labor costs, and R&D synergy by technology and expertise. Individual assets and liabilities acquired and transferred will be evaluated at market value in accompaniment of the business combination and, in addition, goodwill or a negative goodwill will be recognized. In this case, the ground for evaluation of intangible assets and goodwill will therefore be required.

3 Revaluation in the Case of Share Transfer of Daiichi Sankyo Company Limited[2]

The share transfer exchange ratio in this business combination in the first phase was calculated by Merrill Lynch on the basis of the multiple of corporate value share price earnings, which is the multiple of earnings before interest, taxes, and amortization (EBITDA), the discounted cash flow analysis method, comparative company analysis, and contribution analysis.

As the result, the share transfer ratio is one ordinary share of Sankyo Company Limited for one share of Daiichi Sankyo Company

Limited and one share of Daiichi Pharmaceutical Co. Ltd. for 1.159 shares of Daiichi Sankyo Company Limited.[3] First, I carry out discounted cash flow analysis to evaluate the scope of the present value per ordinary share of Daiichi Pharmaceutical Co. Ltd., assuming that Daiichi Pharmaceutical Co. Ltd. will continue its business as an independent company. Calculation was made by Merrill Lynch by the total of discounted net present value of free cash flow[4] for five terms, i.e., from the business year ending March 31, 2006 to the business year ending March 31, 2010 plus discounted net present value of the final value by applying the range of a growth rate that will continue permanently to the standard EBITDA of Daiichi Pharmaceutical Co. Ltd. for the business year ending March 31, 2010. The range of −0.25% to 0.25% was applied to free cash flow that does not allow for the standard interest bearing liabilities of Daiichi Pharmaceutical Co. Ltd. as a growth rate that will continue to grow permanently, and the range of the discount ratio of 4.0% to 6.0% was used for the purpose of calculation.

Merrill Lynch produced a direct price range of 2,530 yen to 3,140 yen using the multiple method of EBITDA in the range of 6.5 times to 8.5 times per ordinary share of Daiichi Pharmaceutical Co. Ltd. and that of 3,042 yen to 4,587 yen using the permanently continuing growth rate method on the basis of this analysis. In the same way, Merrill Lynch produced a direct price range of 2,399 yen to 3,017 yen using the multiple method of EBITDA in the range of 6.5 times to 8.5 times per ordinary share of Daiichi Pharmaceutical Co. Ltd. and that of 2,782 yen to 4,243 yen using the permanently continuing growth rate method.

In the second phase, the total of the number of shares of 439,498,765 of Sankyo Company Limited multiplied by 1 and the number of shares of 286,453,235 of Daiichi Pharmaceutical Co. Ltd. multiplied by 1.159 being 331,999,299 as of the record date of the calculation of the number of shares (March 31, 2005), which was 735,011,343, became the number of shares to be issued.[5]

In the third phase, the purchase price from Daiichi Pharmaceutical Co. Ltd. was determined. The estimated purchase price is 746,462 million yen, comprising 331,999,299 shares times the share price of

2,393 yen as of the announcement day of share transfer and an estimated transaction cost.

In the fourth phase, the part of assets is revalued at market value in the purchase method to reflect the results of the evaluation method of shares in revaluation of assets.

4 Verification of Reasonability of Accounting for Goodwill

Two points under this title follow. First, the difference from the amounts allocated as assets and liabilities that the merging company has acquired and assigned from the merged company will be recognized[6] as goodwill. However, goodwill that the merged company had accounted for under assets before the business combination date may not be recognized.[7] The goodwill of Daiichi Pharmaceutical Co. Ltd. amounting to 5,914 million yen has been written off at one time.

Second, the excess amounting to 28,035 million yen obtained by subtracting assigned liabilities from the part of newly issued capital (share purchase value) plus a fair market value after revaluation of acquired assets in the purchase method is recorded as goodwill. This is an aggregation of economic values that were unable to be revalued in the business combination such as sales network, innovative technology of production, and brand value. I looked up the nature of assets of goodwill of International Accounting Standards Board (IASB).

According to IASB, with assets, economic benefit is expected to flow into an enterprise in the framework as resources controlled by an enterprise as a result of past and future events. IASB mentions that future economic benefit embodied in assets is potential that will contribute to flows of cash and cash equivalents directly or indirectly. IASB concluded that core goodwill represents resources whose future economic benefit is expected to flow into an enterprise.[8]

The corporate reorganization of Daiichi Sankyo Company Limited was carried out in two phases. The first phase was the establishment of a joint holding company at the time of business combination that took place in October 2005, and Daiichi Pharmaceutical Co. Ltd. and Sankyo Company Limited became wholly owned subsidiaries of the holding company (Daiichi Sankyo Company Limited). In the second phase, this joint holding company was made a business holding company centering on medical products, under which overseas subsidiaries were placed. The effect of this sales synergy is shown below. (Please refer to Figure 4 from Figure 1.)

The first sales synergy was that new members were employed when Sankyo Company Limited and Daiichi Pharmaceutical Co. Ltd. were combined, which had a bottom-up effect on the number of MRs in the US market.

By location segment,[9] the overseas sales increased by 59,236 million yen over the previous year.

The second sales synergy is that Sankyo Company Limited is strong in the circulation organ domain for chronic diseases and Daiichi Pharmaceutical Co. Ltd. is strong in infectious disease remedies for acute diseases, and that they can have supplemental sales synergy.

	N. America	Europe	Others	Total
Overseas sales (in million yen)	182,614	98,440	26,210	307,264
Overseas sales/consolidated sales (%)	19.7	10.6	2.9	33.2

Fig. 1   Daiichi Sankyo Company Limited (from April 1, 2005 to March 31, 2006).

	N. America	Europe	Others	Total
Overseas sales (in million yen)	241,850	84,327	30,523	356,700
Overseas sales/consolidated sales (%)	26	9.1	3.3	38.4

Fig. 2   Daiichi Sankyo Company Limited (from April 1, 2006 to March 31, 2007).

	N. America	Europe	Others	Total
Change on last year (in million yen)	59,236	−14,113	4,313	49,436
Increase on last year (%)	32.4	−14.3	16.5	16.1

Fig. 3   Daiichi Sankyo Company Limited (from March 31, 2006 to March 31, 2007).

This can be confirmed by the gross profit margin. The improvement effect on the gross profit margin is estimated to be 648.6 billion yen for the seven terms from the year ending March 2006 to the year ending March 2012 with the year ending March 2005 being the base year.

Thirdly, the improvement effect on the operating income ratio by cost synergy is estimated to be 424.4 billion yen for the seven terms from the year ending March 2006 to the year ending March 2012 with the year ending March 2005 being the base year.

5 Details of R&D Expenditures and Revaluation of Intangible Assets

5.1 *M&A and motive for innovation*

While the added value ratios by industry are 23.1% for steels, 23.6% for electronic equipment parts, 37.6% for information service, 17.2% for food products, 17.9% for automobiles, 19.3% for all industries, and the ratio for medical products is high at 36.0%. The source of the high added value lies in that the ratio of R&D expenditures to sales is high[11] at 8.43% compared to 3.13% for software and data-processing business, 5.05% for electric machinery appliance industry, 3.66% for general chemistry and chemical textile industry, 4.63% for automobile industry, 1.06% for food industry, and 2.98% for all industries.

The following survey[12] can confirm that M&A is carried out with R&D as its motive. This survey focuses on what factor respondents consider important and where M&A is carried out with a motive relating to innovation. The scores of the response are evaluated for five phases from 0, which means "hardly important," through 4, which means "very important." Out of these, the ratios are shown below by classifying the response at 3 or over collectively as "very important." According to the list below, very high ratios of such motive are acquisition of technological resources from a target company at 41.9%, economy of the scope of R&D expenditures at 35.5%, extension of risk of R&D expenditures at 16.1%, and economy of the size of R&D expenditures at 16.1%.

Consolidated accounting year	Mar. 2004	Mar. 05	Mar. 06	Mar. 07	Mar. 08	Mar. 09	Mar. 10	Mar. 11	Mar. 12
Sales	9,191	9,163	9,259	9,295	8,760	8,650	9,460	9,780	10,730
Cost of sales	3,324	3,147	2,907	2,652	2,154	2,029	2,115	2,112	2,190
Gross sales profit	5,867	6,016	6,352	6,643	6,606	6,621	7,345	7,668	8,540
Gross profit margin	63.8%	65.7%	68.6%	71.5%	75.4%	76.5%	77.6%	78.4%	79.6%
Improvement effect on gross profit margin			2.9%	5.8%	9.8%	10.9%	12.0%	12.7%	13.9%
Improvement effect on gross profit margin (single year)			273	540	855	942	1,134	1,247	1,495
Improvement effect on gross profit margin (accumulation)			273	813	1,668	2,610	3,744	4,991	6,486
Operating income	1,417	1,410	1,547	1,363	1,680	1,800	2,300	2,500	3,200
Operating income ratio	15.4%	15.4%	16.7%	14.7%	19.2%	20.8%	24.3%	25.6%	29.8%
Improvement effect on operating income ratio			1.3%	-0.7%	3.8%	5.4%	8.9%	10.2%	14.4%
Improvement effect on operating income ratio (single year)			122	-67	332	469	844	995	1,549
Improvement effect on operating income ratio (accumulation)			122	55	387	856	1,700	2,695	4,244

Fig. 4 Business combination accounting (Analysis of Daiichi Sankyo Company Limited).[10]

Indicate the importance of motives relating to the following technological innovation.

Technology related	Negligible importance[a]		Great importance[b]	
	0	(1, 2)	3	4
1. Economics of scale in R&D		71.0%		16.1%
2. Economics of *scope* in R&D		61.3%		35.5%
3. Restructuring of R&D		67.7%		9.7%
4. Access to technological resources		48.4%		41.9%
5. Access to technological resources in target's environment		58.1%		19.4%
6. R&D risk spreading		77.4%		16.1%
7. Reduce the risk of being imitated		77.4%		3.2%
8. Impose a comment standard		80.6%		0.0%
9. Get competing technologies under control		77.4%		6.5%

Notes:
a. A score equal to 0 indicates negligible importance.
b. A score equal to or greater than 3 indicates great importance.

Fig. 5   M&A motivations: relevance.[13]

5.2   *Examination of reasonability of appropriation*

First, intangible assets are purchased, internally developed, or
acquired by business combination. Intangible assets in business combination are covered by provisions of FAS-141. A fair value will be
allocated to R&D costs obtained by the purchase method in business
combination in relation to the existing GAAP in accordance with
APB16 (business combination).[14] For example, details of accounting
for assets relating to R&D expenditures in the corporate reorganization of Daiichi Sankyo Company Limited are as follows.

On revaluation of intangible fixed assets, 338.0 billion yen comprising 297.0 billion yen of completed technologies and 41.0 billion
yen of patents was recorded as intangible assets. Calculation was
made, allowing for items including change in royalties due to the
maturity of patents on the basis of the instruction of senior managers
of Daiichi Pharmaceutical Co. Ltd. The amount of intangible assets
of 338.0 billion yen was decided on the basis of estimated revenue
from products and operating income concerning a number of products in the next five years and what the company itself has learnt

through a wide range of experience in the medical product industry. If the amount of the final evaluation expected to be completed within 6 to 12 months from the completion of share transfer is different from 338.0 billion yen, identifiable assets are estimated to be adjusted to that amount.

Secondly, with respect to acquisition of technological resources of a target company as an M&A motive, R&D costs currently in progress may contribute to substantial part of purchase prices allocated before a technology company is acquired. The acquiring company has a clear incentive in that the purchase prices of R&D in progress may be allocated to intangible assets. The reason is that the fact that recovery with cash flows is measurable suggests that the probability of generating future profits is high by growth of already launched products and examination of the possibility of commercialization of products in Phase III of the clinical development phase.

It can be said that it is the economy of the scope of R&D expenditures. Anti-thrombosis drugs, arteriosclerosis treatment drug, and drug for the treatment of diabetic neural disease of Sankyo Company Limited are in Phase III; however, anti-thrombosis drug of Daiichi Pharmaceutical Co. Ltd. is in Phase II. The scope of economy can be gained by reviewing development items for which a large R&D expenditure is required.

Third, the economy of the size of R&D expenditures is examined. R&D expenditures amounting to 150.0 billion yen per annum are normally required to be ranked with medical product makers in the world. The ratio of R&D expenditures to sales of Daiichi Sankyo Company Limited is high in the range of 17% to 20% and the ratio of R&D expenditures to gross profit on sales is 25%. Compared to this, R&D expenditures of Takeda Pharmaceutical Co. Ltd. amount to 150.0 billion yen per annum, the ratio of R&D expenditures to sales is in the range of 13% to 14%, and the ratio of R&D expenditures to gross profit on sales is 17%. This indicates that M&A was carried out to secure sales or gross profit on sales that exceeded a certain level.

Fourth, exports of Sankyo Company Limited to the States will decline because a patent for a cholesterol lowering drug expires in April 2006, but Sankyo Company Limited will be able to cover them with sales of Daiichi Pharmaceutical Co. Ltd. by carrying out M&A.

Fifth, "drug manufacturing companies are required to maximize a product by carrying out a number of researches for commercialization from a development phase or accumulating evidence through clinical research after marketing on a large scale. The average sales of 70 products of the top 10 products in terms of sales of the seven domestic drug manufacturers (Eisai Co. Ltd., Sankyo Company Limited, Daiichi Pharmaceutical Co. Ltd., Takeda Pharmaceutical Co. Ltd., Fujisawa Pharmaceutical Co. Ltd., Shionogi Co. Ltd., and Yamanouchi Seiyaku) is 18.93 billion yen and the average product age is 12.8 years. The average product age of 32 growth products is 9.0 years and the average product age of 38 matured products is 16.0 years."[15]

Then, the number of patents held will become an M&A motive. The numbers of patents granted in the States (US-granted) are 732 of Takeda Pharmaceutical Co. Ltd., 254 of Eisai Co. Ltd., and 190 of Shionogi & Co. Ltd., which are on the line of independence and expand sales and profits on their own without experiencing any major merger. At the same time, the number of patents of companies that have carried out major mergers are 324 of Daiichi Sankyo Company Limited, 395 of Astellas Pharma Inc., 254 of Tanabe Mitsubishi Pharmaceutical Co. Ltd. (two companies combined), and 124 of Dainippon Sumitomo Pharma Co. Ltd. (two companies combined).

	United States		Japan
Name of company	Granted	Application	Application
Takeda Pharmaceutical Co. Ltd.	732	48	0
Tanabe Pharmaceutical Co. Ltd.	85	35	281
Mitsubishi Well Pharma Corporation	169	44	190
Tanabe Mitsuibishi Pharmaceutical Co. Ltd.	0	0	0
Dainippon Pharma Co. Ltd.	34	0	0
Sumitomo Pharma Co. Ltd.	90	0	0
Dainippon Sumitomo Pharma Co. Ltd.	0	14	71
Daiichi Sankyo Company Limited.	324	0	0
Fujisawa Pharmaceutical Co. Ltd.	230	122	0
Yamanouchi Seiyaku	91	0	0
Astellas Pharma Inc.	395	0	0
Eisai Co. Ltd.	254	156	506
Shionogi & Co. Ltd.	190	0	0

Fig. 6   The number of patents of major drug manufacturers.[16]

Y	X		
Sales (in 100 million yen)	R&D expenditures (in 100 million yen)	Regression coefficient	6.140469
Sales (in 100 million yen)	R&D expenditures (in 100 million yen)	Correlation coefficient	0.983986
R&D expenditures (in 100 million yen)	Granted	Correlation coefficient	0.878349

Fig. 7   Correlation coefficient between sales and R&D expenditures.

Name of company	Granted	Sales (in million yen)	R&D expenditures (in million yen)
Takeda Pharmaceutical Co. Ltd.	732	13,052	1,933
Tanabe Pharmaceutical Co. Ltd.	85	1,755	285
Mitsubishi Well Pharma Corporation	169	2,275	472
Dainippon Sumitomo Pharma Co. Ltd.	122	2,612	409
Daiichi Sankyo Company Limited.	324	9,295	1,707
Astellas Pharma Inc.	716	9,206	1,679
Eisai Co. Ltd.	254	6,741	1,083
Shionogi & Co. Ltd.	190	2,150	410

Fig. 8   Sales and R&D expenditures.

By looking at the results in more detail, it can be confirmed that the number of patents can become a motive of M&A from the fact that the following results were obtained.

Sixth, change of control (clause of capital control) does not exist in the development projects will become intangible assets as a negative factor that has to be considered in evaluation of M&A. Change of control means an agreement that contains an arrangement such as immediate cancellation of a licensing agreement or immediate repayment of a loan at the time of change in shareholders of a corporation or replacement of management. Change of control originates from a range of preventive measures against hostile acquisition. However, because of the right of control where such license is provided, the provider can cancel the agreement and he or she requires change where M&A such as a merger and stock exchange or where a joint corporation is established by such company and another company.

6 In-Process R&D Expenses

6.1 *What are in-process R&D expenses?*

In-process R&D expenses in M&A are assets used for specific R&D activities. In-process R&D in M&A has the following critical mind toward change.

Evaluation arising from the scene of research or research in an internal project cannot be recognized as intangible assets at the time of business combination. The reason is that expenses for research or an internal project must be accounted as costs when they are incurred.

It is impossible to prove that what arises from a scene of research in an internal project has intangible assets from which an acquisition enterprise is highly likely to create economic benefits, which is a requirement of assets. Accordingly, in any scene, it is recognized as costs when incurred.

6.2 *M&A of Eisai Co. Ltd. and Takeda Pharmaceutical Co. Ltd.*

In-process R&D expenses can be seen in the M&A cases of Eisai Co. Ltd. and Takeda Pharmaceutical Co., Ltd. in Japan. Eisai Co. Ltd. acquired MGI Pharma in the United States for 400.0 billion yen in January 2008, making its wholly owned subsidiary and it amortized US$840 million (80.0 billion yen) of in-process R&D expenses at one time. However, the company regularly takes an impairment test on goodwill amounting to US$1,744 million incurred without amortizing it.

Cash generating power indicates financial activities usable for growth investment, investment activities of business development, dividend payment, and loan repayment. Accordingly, cash flow for operating activities is represented in an equation of net income + depreciation/amortization costs of tangible and intangible assets + in-process R&D expenses + goodwill amortization costs + impairment loss.

Next, Takeda Pharmaceutical Co. Ltd. acquired shares of Millennium Pharmaceuticals Inc., a US biomedical products company. This was carried out through a merger of US Jaguar Acquisition Corporation, a consolidated subsidiary of Takeda Pharmaceutical Co. Ltd. and Millennium Pharmaceuticals Inc. by the purchase method. The acquisition price is US$3,944 million and the distribution to assets is represented by US$1,378 million of intangible fixed assets (value of products and technologies), Δ US$551 million (Δ 4.5 billion yen) of deferred tax liabilities on this, US$840 million of in-process R&D expenses (value of development products) (87.4 billion yen of R&D expenses), and US$533 million of other asset liability. The goodwill is US$1,744 million and it will be amortized over 20 years due to the application of the Japanese accounting standards, "Integration of Accounting Treatment of Overseas Subsidiaries." Profit and loss will be affected by goodwill amortization, but cash flow will not be affected.

6.3   Direction of in-process R&D expenses

Under US accounting standards, all in-process R&D expenses are amortized at one time as costs in the year in which they are incurred. Financial Accounting Standards Board (FASB) and IASB have recently developed a joint project of an exposure draft common for accounting of business combination.[17]

First, there are two requirements that in-process R&D should be recognized by differentiating from goodwill and intangible assets. The first point is legal grounds. Where intangible assets are created by an agreement or law; they will be differentiated from goodwill, as rights of intangible assets are transferable. The second point is separate ability. They are cases where intangible assets are not created by an agreement or other legal rights and they are separable and the separation, sale, transfer, provision of a license, renting, or exchange can be made from the acquired enterprise. In-process R&D is an asset that is used for the purpose of specific research activities; it cannot be used for any other purpose in future and it represents an amount arisen from R&D, out of an amount of difference between the acquired price and the amount of net assets of an enterprise.

Second, the FASB issued public draft 204-00 to amend accounting standards of business combination on January 30, 2005. The public draft amends Paragraph 16 of SFAS2 "Accounting for Research and Development Costs." An unrestricted number of years of useful life should be considered for intangible assets, which are acquired in business combination to use for a specific R&D project and they do not have replacing future users, until the effects of their relevant R&D is completed or abandoned. Managers determine whether this project has succeeded, failed, or it is continuing as process R&D in every accounting period. Where the project has succeeded, the number of years of useful life of project process R&D intangible assets is reasonably forecast and the profits available from the project correspond to amortization costs from process R&D assets. Where the project fails, the process R&D assets shall be declared an impairment loss.

7 Conclusion

R&D expenses are made deductible because there is no direct relationship between input and production. However, business combination accounting has overcome this by a new market value concept, DCF, by counting the purchase of assets as expense. In this paper, I have justified it based on of the examples of medical product companies.

In-process R&D expenses by M&A are expenses for accounting purposes under current Japanese standards, but deferred tax liabilities are incurred in tax effect accounting because they are excluded from expenses for taxation purposes. In addition, there is not fund outflow of in-process R&D expenses by M&A in cash flow. It is therefore necessary to research their effects on share prices. Simultaneously, if they are once accounted as intangible assets on the basis of success or failure of the project in accordance with Item 3 of IFRS, arbitrariness will occur unless a project has a high probability of commercialization such as a clinical development phase (Phase 3) so that accounting for impairment loss caused by its failure may not become arbitrary.

Notes

[1] Richard G. sloan, Do stock prices reflect information in accruals and cash flows about future earnings, *The Accounting Review*, vol. 71, no. 3 (July 1996), pp. 289–315.

[2] For this section, I have translated joint share transfer of shares of Daiichi Pharmaceutical Co. Ltd. and Sankyo Company Limited, for Shares of Daiichi Sankyo Company Limited (2006) and they have taken out data therefrom.

[3] From "Securities Reports" of Sankyo Company Limited and Daiichi Pharmaceutical Co. Ltd.

[4] Here, free cash flow does not allow for interest bearing liabilities.

[5] Accurately, the number of shares in issue as of the record day on which the number of shares is calculated less the number of own shares eliminated by Sankyo Company Limited and Daiichi Pharmaceutical Co. Ltd. on and after the day following that record day plus the number of ordinary shares newly issued due to an exercise of subscription warrants.

[6] FASB, SFAS141 Business Combination, par. 43.

[7] FASB, SFAS141 Business Combination, par. 38.

[8] IFRS3, Business Combinations-BC132.

[9] The author calculated on the basis of the figures from "Securities Report" (fiscal 2007) of Daiichi Sankyo Company Limited.

[10] Estimated figures of business performance prepared on the basis of Financial Economic Research Institute in the medical product sector; report prepared by Nomura Securities were used as estimated figures of sales, gross profit on sales, and operating income for March 2008 to March 2012 in this analysis and the analysis was independently made by the author.

[11] "Science and Technology Research Survey Report" published by the Ministry of Internal Affairs and Communications.

[12] "Mergers and acquisitions — the innovation impact" by Cassiman and Colombo and it is published in 2006 by Edward Elgar.

[13] Ibid, p. 101.

[14] FASB, Interpretation No. 4 "Applicability of Purchase method," pars. 4 and 5.

[15] "Medicine Industry Research Institute Policy Research News" in "Product Age in the Pharmaceutical Product Market in Japan and the USA," No. 16, February 2005, pp. 8–10.

[16] Source: Thomson Scientific, Delphion, 2007.

References

Cassiman, B and MG Colombo (2006). *Mergers and Acquisitions – The Innovation Impact*, Edward Elgar.

Joint Share Transfer of Shares of Daiichi Pharmaceutical Co. Ltd. and Sankyo Company Limited, Limited for Shares of Daiichi Sankyo Company Limited, Limited (2006).

Slavin, NS and AR Khan (2006). In-process R&D in business acquisitions – more disclosure needed for transparency and comparability, *The CPA Journal*, 76, 58–63.

The International Financial Reporting Group of Young. *Generally Accepted Accounting Practice under International Financial Reporting Standards 2007/2008*. Lexis Nexis (translation in Japanese by Ernst & Young).

3

The Method of Payment in Takeovers and Earnings Management

Kunimaru Takahashi

Professor, Faculty of Business Administration, Aoyama Gakuin University

1 Introduction

This study investigates the impact of a takeover on management incentives to increase reported earnings. Takeovers in Japan have been increasing since the second half of the 1990s. Indeed, according to merger and acquisition (M&A) services provider RECOF Co., the 15 trillion yen spent on takeovers in 2006 exceeded all R&D expenditure by Japanese companies. One explanation for the increased level of takeover activity in Japan has been the result of legislation in 1999, which was designed to promote takeovers and, by fostering efficient capital reallocation, revitalize the economy. For example, since October 1999, the stock exchange has permitted the acquisition of all shares in a company in exchange for stock without the need for cash. Stock transfers also allow companies to establish a holding company to facilitate business combinations. Further, since April 2001, companies have been permitted to transfer all or part of their business more speedily before they are substantially ruined (Higgins and Beckman, 2006).

Companies engage in takeovers to create a shareholder value greater than the sum of the companies involved. Previous studies have found that takeovers appear to create shareholder value. Andrade, Mitchell, and Stafford (2001), for instance, undertook a comprehensive analysis of the combined returns of a sample of 3,688 takeovers by US companies from 1973 to 1998. They found that the combined average cumulative abnormal return (CAR) over the three-day window $(-1, +1)$ around the takeover announcement was 1.8%, suggesting that takeovers, on average, create shareholder value. They also found that bidders do not post any significant returns, while targets experience significant positive returns. To better understand the effects of takeovers, previous studies have measured how various factors affect the magnitude of returns; several possible explanations exist. In particular, Huang and Walking (1987) and Sirower (1997) found that the most powerful influence on takeover returns was the method of payment.

An acquiring firm can use two basic methods to pay for an acquisition: cash or stock. Several existing studies have shown the effects of the method of payment on the return to both acquiring and target firms. Andrade, Mitchell, and Stafford (2001) found that the average acquiring firm return with a stock transaction for the period 1973 to 1998 was -1.5%, while the average acquiring firm return in a cash transaction was 0.4%. It was insignificantly different from zero. As with the analysis of targets, target firm shareholders also do better when there is no equity financing. The average target firm's return in a stock transaction over three days was 13% and the average target firm's return in a cash transaction was just over 20%. These results suggest that the method of payment has a significant impact on value creation in takeovers.

Inoue (2002) examined 137 acquiring firms and 147 target firms publicly traded in Japan and he compared the difference between the abnormal returns before and after the enactment of the new legislation in 1999. He examined the takeover effects by transaction type on stock returns and found that the CARs for the acquiring and target firms before enactment of the new legislation over a three-day window $(-1, +1)$ around the takeover announcement were -1.19% and 1.06%, respectively. Conversely, the CARs for acquiring and target firms following enactment of the new legislation were 3.01% and 5.97%, respectively. Inoue (2002) further classified the transaction type into four categories — mergers, takeover bids (TOB), stock-for-stock exchanges, and stock transfers — and compared the differences between the abnormal returns following enactment of the new legislation. The CARs for the acquiring and target firms were found to be significantly different from zero in a stock-for-stock exchange and stock transfers while the CARs for the acquiring firms were not significantly different from zero in TOB.

On this basis, Inoue (2002) concluded that transaction costs decreased because under the new legislation, managers could select the type of takeover and consequently stock-for-stock exchange and stock transfer firms showed significant positive abnormal returns after 1999. This is because, for takeovers, where the consideration received by the target shareholders is the stock of the acquiring firm, an exchange ratio agreed upon by the acquiring and target firms determines the total number of issued shares. Because this exchange ratio relates to the acquiring and target firms' stock prices, the managers of both firms have a strong incentive to increase earnings.

The remainder of the paper is organized as follows. Section 2 provides a summary of previous research on the relationship between takeovers and earnings management; Section 3 outlines the research design, sample, and data sources; Section 4 presents the results; and Section 5 concludes.

2   Earnings Management and Takeovers

Earnings management is the choice by a manager of accounting policies to achieve some particular objective (Scott, 2003). Previous researchers have studied specific events such as initial public offers (Teoh *et al.*, 1998a,b; Friedlan, 1994), management buyouts (DeAngelo, 1986; Perry and Williams, 1994), and proxy contests (DeAngelo, 1988) on management incentives to increase or decrease reported earnings. However, there are few studies of the effect of takeovers on earnings management.

Christie and Zimmerman (1994) measured accounting opportunism by comparing the frequency of the choice of income-increasing procedures by takeover targets with the corresponding frequency of their surviving industry peers. They found that takeover targets selected income-increasing depreciation, inventory, and investment tax credits (ITC) more frequently than their surviving peers in the years leading up to a control action. Groff and Wright (1989) found almost the same results as Christie and Zimmerman (1994). These studies, however, have certain limitations when considering earnings management: namely, they all employ a single accounting method (depreciation, inventory, and investment tax credits) for measuring accounting opportunism.

In contrast to the studies that use a single accounting method, recent studies examining the relation between earnings management and takeovers employ the Jones model or modified Jones model. For example, using the modified Jones model, Erickson and Wang (1999) investigated whether acquiring firms manipulated accounting earnings upwards prior to stock-for-stock mergers. They found that acquiring firms attempted to manage earnings upward in the period before the merger agreement. Erickson and Wang, however, found no evidence of earnings management by target firms. Consistent with Erickson and Wang, Louis (2004) found strong evidence suggesting that acquiring firms overstate their earnings for the quarter prior to the takeover announcement.

In contrast to Erickson and Wang (1999) and Louis (2004), some other studies consider only earnings management by target firms (Easterwood, 1998; Eddy and Taylor, 1999; North and O'Connell, 2002; Koumanakos *et al.*, 2005). For example, Eddy and Taylor investigated whether Australian target firms manage their earnings during takeover bids. They found that although the target firms displayed negative abnormal accruals, the results were not statistically significant. Alternatively, Easterwood provides evidence that takeover targets systematically increase their earnings during the quarter immediately preceding initiation of the takeover attempt.

Therefore, previous research on the relation between takeovers and earnings management has found mixed results and most studies, with the exception of Erickson and Wang (1999) and Louis (2004), have only examined the relationship in target firms.

3   Research Design and Sample Selection

3.1   *Measurement of earnings management*

This study investigates whether the managers of acquiring and target firms have a strong incentive to increase earnings in stock-for-stock mergers around the agreed-on exchange ratio. As previously discussed, Christie and Zimmerman (1994) and Groff and Wright (1989) use a single accounting method for detecting earnings management. However, most previous studies examining the relation between earnings management and takeovers use the Jones model or modified Jones model. The Jones model is the most widely used in studies of aggregate accruals. Watts and Zimmerman (1990) note that accruals-based measures are theoretically appealing because they aggregate into a single measure the net effect of many recognition and measurement decisions, thereby capturing the portfolio nature of income determination. Therefore, this study adopts a cross-sectional modified Jones model that is consistently able to detect earnings management. This model calculates abnormal accruals by running cross-sectional regressions on a sample of firms in the same two-digit standard industrial classification (SIC) code as the acquiring or target firm while excluding the sample firm. The cross-sectional estimation of the modified Jones model takes the following form:

$$TA_{ijt}/AST_{ijt-2} = \beta_{0jt}[1/AST_{ijt-2}]$$
$$+ \beta_{1ijt}[(\Delta REV_{ijt} - \Delta REC_{ijt})/AST_{ijt-2}]$$
$$+ \beta_{2jt}[PPE_{ijt}/AST_{ijt-2}] + \varepsilon_{ijt} \qquad (1)$$

where:

TA_{ijt} = total accruals for estimation of portfolio j for firm i in event period t;

ΔREV_{ijt} = change in revenue for estimation of portfolio j for firm i in event period t;

PPE_{ijt} = gross property, plant, and equipment for estimation of portfolio j for firm i in event period t;

AST_{ijt-2} = beginning of period total assets for estimation of portfolio j for firm i in event period t;

ε_{ijt} = error term for estimation of portfolio j for firm i in event period t, where $i = 1, \ldots, N$ for the firm index, $j = 1, \ldots, J$ for the portfolio index, and $t = 1, \ldots, T$ for the half-year index (for years included in the event period).

The estimated discretionary accruals are:

$$DAT_{it} = TA_{it}/AST_{it-2} - [b_{0it}(1/AST_{it-2}) + b_{1jt}(\Delta REV_{it}/AST_{it-2}$$
$$- \Delta REC_{it}/AST_{it-2}) + b_{2jt}(PPE_{ijt}/AST_{ijt-2})] \qquad (2)$$

Equation 1 allows for a true constant term in the regression. To reduce heteroskedasticity, lagged total assets are used to scale all variables.

In addition to total accruals, we calculate working capital accruals. Working capital accruals exclude depreciation from total accruals. As Louis (2004) argues, long-term accruals (such as depreciation and amortization), do not account for variation in total accruals and these accruals are less susceptible to manipulation. We estimate the following working capital accrual model:

$$WCA_{ijt}/AST_{ijt-2} = \gamma_{0jt}[1/AST_{ijt-2}] + \gamma_{1jt}$$
$$\times [(\Delta REV_{ijt} - \Delta REC_{ijt})/AST_{ijt-2}] + \varepsilon_{ijt}$$
$$(3)$$

where:

WCA_{ijt} = working capital accruals for estimation of portfolio j for firm i in event period t, and estimated discretionary working capital accruals are computed as:

$$DAW_{it} = WCA_{it}/AST_{it-2} - [c_{0jt}(1/AST_{it-2})$$
$$+ c_{1jt}(\Delta REV_{it}/AST_{it-2} - \Delta REC_{it}/AST_{it-2})] \qquad (4)$$

3.2 Sample

Using the database on takeovers prepared by RECOF Co., the Japanese M&A services provider, the initial sample comprises 392 publicly traded Japanese firms involved in stock-for-stock mergers and 116 firms involved in cash mergers between October 1, 1999 and June 30, 2006. Effective from October 1999, the vehicle for stock-for-stock exchange allows the acquisition of all of the shares of another company using stock without the need for cash. In addition, effective from October 1999, the vehicle for stock transfers allows companies to establish a holding company to facilitate business combinations. Therefore, we collected and used the sample period after October 1, 1999. Both successful and unsuccessful takeover attempts are included in this sample. The takeover announcement and scheduled dates are from MARR (Merger Acquisition Research Report published by RECOF Co.). Financial data are from the Nikkei Economic Electronic Databank System — Financial QUEST online database service.

Easterwood (1998) provides evidence that takeover targets systematically increase their earnings during the quarter immediately preceding initiation of the takeover attempt. Furthermore, she split the sample between hostile and friendly takeovers and she examined the discretionary accruals of these groups separately. Bivariate tests indicated that the result was statistically significant for targets of hostile takeovers, but not for targets of friendly takeovers. Therefore, we should consider the effect of a hostile takeover on the amount of discretionary accruals. However, as there are only a few hostile takeovers during the sample period, they are excluded from the analysis. Eliminating firms without the complete takeover and accounting data necessary for the analysis results in a final sample of 203 firms involved in stock-for-stock mergers and 95 firms in cash mergers. In the stock-for-stock merger sample, 123 firms are acquirers and 80 are targets. In the cash merger sample, 45 firms are acquirers and 50 are targets.

Erickson and Wang (1999), Easterwood (1998), and Louis (2004) used quarterly financial statement information for their respective analyses. However, the Financial QUEST online database does not provide sufficient quarterly financial statement information between October 1, 1999 and June 30, 2006. For this reason, we use half-year financial statement information in the analysis.

Erickson and Wang (1999) define the stock-for-stock merger process as follows: negotiating the terms of the transaction, reaching an agreement, and completing the exchange of the acquiring firm's stock for the target's stock or assets. The managers of the acquiring firms and the target firms then have an opportunity to increase reported earnings in the half year preceding the agreed-on exchange ratio in the merger. Therefore, for stock-for-stock merger sample firms, the half year with an earnings release immediately preceding the agreed-on exchange ratio of the merger is half-year t. The first half year preceding half-year t is then defined as half-year $t-1$ and the first half year succeeding half-year t is defined as half-year $t+1$. In contrast, there is no need to agree on the exchange ratio for cash mergers. For this reason, in the cash merger sample, the half year with an earnings release immediately preceding the merger announcement date is half-year t.

4   Results

4.1   *Descriptive statistics*

Figure 1 presents descriptive statistics for the sample of acquiring and target firms, including total assets, half-year sales, half-year earnings, return on assets, free cash flow, and debt. Free cash flow and debt are divided by total assets at the end of the fiscal half year immediately preceding the agreed-on exchange ratio of the merger in the stock-for-stock merger sample. For the cash merger sample, free cash flow and debt are divided by total assets at the end of the fiscal half year with an earnings release immediately preceding the merger announcement date. Panel A presents statistics for the samples of the acquiring firms. The T-test and Wilcoxon Rank Sum test are used to test for differences between the stock-for-stock and cash merger firms. Panel A indicates that the differences in total assets, half-year sales, and half-year earnings between the stock-for-stock and cash merger firms are statistically significant. This indicates that firms in cash mergers are larger than firms in stock-for-stock mergers. Although the free cash flow to total assets for cash merger firms is larger than in stock-for-stock merger firms, the difference is not statistically significant.

Panel B presents statistics for the sample of target firms. Panel B indicates that differences in total assets, return on assets, and the debt-to-total assets between stock-for-stock and cash merger firms are statistically significant. This indicates that cash merger firms are more profitable and financially sound than stock-for-stock merger firms.

Panel A: The samples of the acquiring firms

	Stock-for-stock mergers		Cash mergers		T-statistic (Wilcoxon Z)	
	Mean	Median	Mean	Median	Mean	Median
Total assets (mil. yen)	420850.4	98693	656907.5	288253	−1.45285	−2.63976***
					(0.14815)	(0.00829)
Sales (mil. yen)	98278.68	14127	287953.7	77615	−2.53614**	−4.31423***
					(0.01311)	(0.00001)
Net income (mil. yen)	730.7155	305	7605.6	755	−1.92905*	−2.79915***
					(0.05971)	(0.00512)
ROA	0.031788	0.043436	0.093637	0.056984	−1.47491	−1.43271
					(0.14213)	(0.15194)
Free-cash-flow to total assets	−0.00603	0.027873	0.021097	0.028922	−0.8081	−0.20595
					(0.42019)	(0.836829)
Debt to total assets	0.484009	0.478183	0.512498	0.511935	−0.68287	−0.66621
					(0.49563)	(0.50527)

***, **, * Significant at 1%, 5%, and 10% level, respectively, using two-tailed *t*-test or Wilcoxon signed-rank test.

Fig. 1　Descriptive statistics: univariate comparisons of the stock-for-stock merger versus cash merger.

Panel B: The samples of the target firms

	Stock-for-stock mergers		Cash mergers		T-statistic (Wilcoxon Z)	
	Mean	Median	Mean	Median	Mean	Median
Total assets (mil. yen)	137868.4	29126.5	57224.52	14694.5	2.00069**	2.63976***
					(0.04776)	(0.00447)
Sales (mil. yen)	63411.61	19669	36952.44	13404	1.24291	4.31423*
					(0.21617)	(0.06611)
Net income (mil. yen)	744.925	79	424.18	162	0.37535	−2.79915
					(0.70801)	(0.26279)
ROA	0.018769	0.015538	0.054182	0.034606	−2.0141*	−1.43271***
					(0.04609)	(0.00447)
Free-cash-flow to total assets	0.141939	0.037228	0.043615	0.024992	0.91417	1.03366
					(0.36234)	(0.30129)
Debt to total assets	0.608139	0.642497	0.512285	0.559667	2.25423**	2.12475**
					(0.0258)	(0.0336)

***, **, * Significant at 1%, 5%, and 10% level, respectively, using two-tailed t-test or Wilcoxon signed-rank test. Free cash flow and debt are divided by total assets at the end of the fiscal half year immediately preceding the agreed-on exchange ratio of the merger in the stock-for-stock merger sample. For the cash merger sample, free cash flow and debt are divided by total assets at the end of the fiscal half year with earnings.

Fig. 1 (*Continued*)

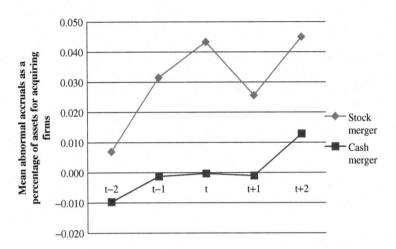

Fig. 2 Plotting of the mean abnormal accruals as a percentage of assets for acquiring firms around the agreed-on exchange ratio of the merger.

4.2   Abnormal accruals for acquiring firms around the agreed-on exchange ratio of the merger

Figure 2 plots the mean abnormal accruals as a percentage of assets for acquiring firms around the agreed-on exchange ratio of the merger. The mean abnormal accruals for the stock-for-stock merger firms are 0.007, 0.03152, and 0.04328 for half years $t - 2$ to t, respectively. The mean abnormal accruals for cash merger firms are -0.00415, -0.00133, and -0.00035 for half years $t - 2$ to t, respectively. As a result, the mean abnormal accruals for stock-for-stock merger firms are higher than the mean abnormal accruals for cash merger firms for half years $t - 2$ to t and the differences between the two groups are statistically significant for half years $t - 1$ and t. This indicates that the managers of acquiring firms in a stock-for-stock merger increase earnings preceding the agreed-on exchange ratio of the merger.

Following Louis (2004) and Botsari and Meek (2008), we conducted additional tests to examine whether working capital items explain this result. Working capital accruals exclude depreciation and amortization from total accruals; therefore, it is easy to understand

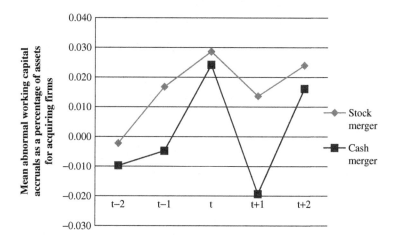

Fig. 3 Plotting of the mean abnormal working capital accruals as a percentage of assets for acquiring firms around the agreed-on exchange ratio of the merger.

whether managers of firms use short-term accruals to manage earnings. In addition, Louis notes that investment bankers rely on earnings before interest, taxes, depreciation, and amortization in valuing acquisition partners. Therefore, the manager of an acquiring firm is more likely to manage working capital accruals.

Figure 3 plots the mean abnormal working capital accruals as a percentage of assets for acquiring firms around the agreed-on exchange ratio of the merger. The mean abnormal working capital accruals in stock-for-stock merger firms are -0.0022, 0.0168, and 0.0287 for half years $t - 2$ to t, respectively, while the mean abnormal working capital accruals for cash merger firms are -0.00966, -0.00474, and 0.02411 for half years $t - 2$ to t, respectively. The mean abnormal working capital accruals for a stock-for-stock merger firm are negative at $t - 2$ and then they increase gradually from $t - 1$ to t. In contrast, the mean abnormal working capital accruals for cash merger firms are negative at $t - 2$ and $t - 1$, but at t, the mean is not negative. While mean abnormal working capital accruals in stock-for-stock merger firms are higher than the mean abnormal working capital accruals for cash merger firms for half years $t - 2$ to t, the differences between the two groups are only statistically significant for half years $t - 1$ and t.

These findings indicate that the managers of acquiring firms in a stock-for-stock merger increase earnings preceding the agreed-on exchange ratio of the merger. We compared the means for the two groups for half years $t - 2$ to t and found that there is a significant difference between the two groups at $t-2$ and $t-1$. This suggests that the managers of firms in a stock-for-stock merger tend to increase earnings preceding the agreed-on exchange ratio of the merger.

4.3 Abnormal accruals for target firms around the agreed-on exchange ratio of the merger

Figure 4 plots the mean abnormal accruals as a percentage of assets for target firms around the agreed-on exchange ratio of the merger. Figure 5 shows univariate comparisons of discretionary accruals for stock versus cash mergers. The mean abnormal accruals for stock-for-stock merger firms are found to be 0.01925, 0.02445, and 0.01357 for half years $t - 2$ to t, respectively, while the mean abnormal accruals for cash merger firms are -0.02982, -0.02872, and 0.00806 for half

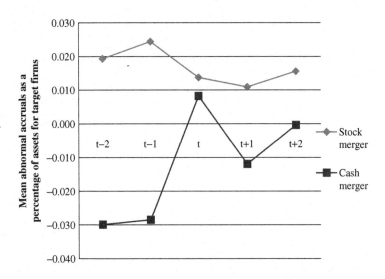

Fig. 4 Plotting of the mean abnormal accruals as a percentage of assets for target firms around the agreed-on exchange ratio of the merger.

Panel A: The samples of the acquiring firms

Stock-for-stock mergers		Cash mergers		T-statistic (Wilcoxon Z)	
Mean	Median	Mean total	Median accruals	Mean	Median
$t-2$ 0.00700	0.00102	−0.00974	−0.00415	1.41696	0.90260
				(0.15991)	(0.36578)
$t-1$ 0.03152	0.00145	−0.00133	−0.00310	2.06639**	1.32880
				(0.04037)	(0.18331)
t 0.04328	0.00499	−0.00035	−0.00733	2.25830**	1.69780*
				(0.02522)	(0.08921)
Working capital accruals					
$t-2$ 0.00222	−0.00434	−0.00966	−0.00258	0.55242	−0.12890
				(0.58140)	(0.89598)
$t-1$ 0.01680	−0.00735	−0.00474	−0.01079	1.42416	0.89900
				(0.15627)	(0.36768)
t 0.02870	−0.00197	0.02411	0.01065	0.25246	−0.45490
				(0.80099)	(0.64790)

**, * Significant at 5% and 10% level, respectively, using two-tailed t-test or Wilcoxon signed-rank test.

Panel B: The samples of the target firms

Stock-for-stock mergers		Cash mergers		T-statistic (Wilcoxon Z)	
Mean	Median	Mean total	Median accruals	Mean	Median
$t-2$ 0.01925	0.00447	−0.02982	−0.00281	2.34704**	1.68690*
				(0.020457)	(0.09116)
$t-1$ 0.02445	0.00960	−0.02872	−0.01502	3.39790**	3.89780***
				(0.00101)	(0.00009)
t 0.01357	−0.00569	0.00806	−0.00288	0.27101	0.66280
				(0.78681)	(0.50593)
Working capital accruals					
$t-2$ 0.00382	−0.00347	−0.02446	−0.01214	1.79570*	1.49785
				(0.07490)	(0.13417)
$t-1$ 0.00516	−0.00177	−0.01830	−0.02058	1.74559*	1.63185
				(0.08328)	(0.10271)
t −0.00731	−0.00729	0.00864	0.00406	−0.73553	−0.97624
				(0.46499)	(0.32894)

***, **, * Significant at 1%, 5%, and 10% level, respectively, using two-tailed t-test or Wilcoxon signed.

Fig. 5   Bivariate results for half year t using the modified Jones model to computing the abnormal accruals.

years $t - 2$ to t, respectively. The mean abnormal accruals in stock-for-stock merger firms are higher than the mean abnormal accruals for cash merger firms for half years $t - 2$ and $t - 1$ and there are significant differences between the two groups for half years $t - 2$ and $t - 1$. As the results for the target firms are almost the same as those for the acquiring firms, we conclude that the managers of target firms in a stock-for-stock merger increase earnings preceding the agreed-on exchange ratio of the merger.

Figure 6 plots the mean abnormal working capital accruals as a percentage of assets for target firms around the agreed-on exchange ratio of the merger. The mean abnormal working capital accruals in stock-for-stock merger firms are 0.00382, 0.00516, and -0.0073 for half years $t - 2$ to t, respectively, and the mean abnormal working capital accruals for cash merger firms are -0.01214, -0.0183, and 0.00864 for half years $t - 2$ to t, respectively. However, while mean abnormal working capital accruals in stock-for-stock merger firms are higher than those for cash merger firms for half years $t - 2$ to $t - 1$, there is no significant difference between the two groups at t. While Erickson and Wang (1999) and Eddy and Taylor (1999) found no statistically significant evidence of earnings management for target firms, these results indicate that the managers of target firms in

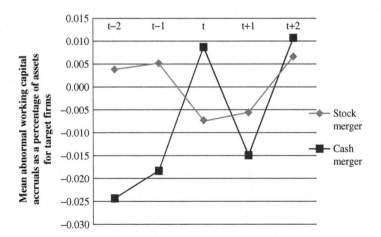

Fig. 6   Plotting of the mean abnormal working capital accruals as a percentage of assets for target firms around the agreed-on exchange ratio of the merger.

a stock-for-stock merger increase earnings preceding the agreed-on exchange ratio of the merger.

5 Conclusion

Following the enactment in 1999 of new legislation in Japan, acquiring firms can use stock to purchase the target firm's stock or assets. North and O'Connell (2002) argue that a key difference between a cash offer and a (risky) securities offer in a takeover is that, unlike cash, the security's value depends on the profitability of the acquisition. Therefore, firm managers have a strong incentive to increase earnings in stock-for-stock mergers around the agreed-on exchange ratio of the merger. Previous research into takeovers has yet to examine the impact of the method of payment on the incentives of the acquiring or target firms' management to manage earnings. However, both the acquiring and target firms' management have an incentive to increase earnings in stock-for-stock mergers.

Erickson and Wang (1999) found that acquiring firms managed earnings upwards during periods prior to the merger agreement, but the abnormal accruals of the target firm were not significantly different from zero. They suggested that the timing of the acquisition caused this finding; acquiring firms can identify and time the acquisition while the target firm is usually unaware of the potential buyout until the acquiring firm initiates negotiations. However, our findings suggest that abnormal accruals are positive and statistically significant for acquiring and target firms in a stock-for-stock merger. Empirical tests indicate that the managers of acquiring and target firms manage earnings upwards prior to the agreed-on exchange ratio of the merger.

Companies engage in takeovers to create a higher shareholder value than the sum of the companies involved. While this paper tests whether acquiring firms create synergies to add to their economic value, we cannot find different synergy effects for the different methods of payment. We need to analyze whether acquiring firms create synergy from takeovers for at least three or five years after the takeover. Further, takeovers within corporate groups in Japan have been increasing since the second half of the 1990s. According to MARR, about 70% of takeover transactions were within a corporate group in 2005. Future research could be undertaken that determines whether takeovers within a corporate group have different effects on management incentives to manage earnings.

References

Andrade, G, M Mitchell and E Stafford (2001). New evidence and perspectives on mergers. *Journal of Economic Perspectives*, 15(2), 103–120.

Botsari, A and G Meek (2008). Do acquirers manage earnings prior to a share for share bid? *Journal of Business Finance & Accounting*, 35(5–6), 633–670.

Christie, A and JL Zimmerman (1994). Efficient and opportunistic choices of accounting procedures. *The Accounting Review*, 69(4), 539–566.

DeAngelo, LE (1986). Accounting numbers as market valuation substitutes. *The Accounting Review*, 61(3), 400–420.

DeAngelo, LE (1988). Managerial competition, information costs, and corporate governance: the use of accounting performance measures in proxy contests. *Journal of Accounting and Economics*, 10, 3–36.

Dechow, PM, RG Sloan and AP Sweeney (1995). Detecting Earnings Management. *The Accounting Review*, 70, 193–225.

Easterwood, CM (1998). Takeovers and incentives for earnings management. *Journal of Applied Business Research*, 14(1), 29–47.

Eddey, PH and SL Taylor (1999). Directors' recommendations on takeover bids and the management of earnings. *Abacus*, 35(1), 29–45.

Erickson, M and S Wang (1999). Earnings management by aquiring firms in stock for stock mergers. *Journal of Accounting and Economics*, 27(2), 149–176.

Friedlan, JM (1994). Accounting choices if issuers of initial public offerings. *Contemporary Accounting Research*, 11, 1–31.

Groff and Wright (1989). The market for corporate control and its implications for accounting policy choice. *Advances in Accounting*, 7, 3–21.

Higgins, HN and J Beckman (2006). Abnormal returns of Japanese acquisition bidders: impact of pro M&A legislation in the 1990s. *Pacific-Basin Finance Journal*, 14(3), 250–268.

Huang, Y and R Walking (1987). Target abnormal returns associated with acquisition announcements — payment, acquisition form and managerial resistance. *Journal of Financial Economics*, 19, 329–349.

Inoue, K (2002). Transaction type and share price impact of Japanese M&As. *Keiei Zaimu Kenkyu*, 22(2), 107–120. (in Japanese).

Koumanakos, E, C Siriopoulos and A Georgopoulos (2005). Firm acquisitions and earnings management: evidence from Greece. *Managerial Auditing Journal*, 20(7), 663–678.

Louis, H (2004). Earnings management and the market performance of acquiring firms. *Journal of Financial Economics*, 74, 121–148.

North, DS and BT O'Connel (2002). Earnings management and mode of payment in takeovers, working paper, University of Richmond, Richmond, VA.

Perry, SE and TH Williams (1994). Earnings management preceding management buyout offers. *Journal of Accounting and Economics*, 18(2), 157–179.

Rappaport and Sirower (1999). Stock or cash? *Harvard Business Review*, Nov–Dec, 147–158.

Schwert, G (2000). Hostility in takeovers. *Journal of Finance*, 55(6), 2599–2640.

Scott, W (2003). *Financial Accounting Theory*, Prentice Hall.

Sirower, ML (1997). *The Synergy Trap: How Companies Lose the Acquisition Game*, Free Press.

Teoh, SH, I Welch and TJ Wong (1998a). Earnings management and the long-run market performance of initial public offerings. *Journal of Finance*, 53, 1935–1974.

Teoh, SH, TJ Wong and G Rao (1998b). Are accruals during initial public offerings opportunistic? *Review of Accounting Studies*, 3, 175–208.

Watts, R and J Zimmerman (1990). Positive accounting theory: a ten-year perspective. *The Accounting Review*, 65, 131–156.

4
Income Smoothing and the Just-in-Time System in the Japanese Automobile Industry

Michio Kunimura

Professor, Department of Business and Management, Meijo University

1 Potential Inventory Manipulation

In this paper, I examine earnings management through real activities of inventory. An increase of inventory does not necessarily lead to an increase in net income. Therefore, I must first show the case of an income increase that occurs when inventory increases. Overproduction sometimes intentionally results in lower cost of goods sold than usual and it increases profit (Roychowdhury, 2006) through lower fixed overhead costs per unit. For example, top management hesitates to stop production lines under a lower level of realized sales than budgetary planned sales and it artificially keeps the production level constant with unwelcome overproduction, that is, with a large amount of unnecessary inventory. In this case, a lower allocation rate of fixed overhead costs than necessary to meet expected demand results in higher inventory costs and higher net income. For instance, if the cost of goods sold is 9,000 units, inventory is 1,000 units (finished goods base) and fixed overhead cost is 1,200 million yen, then the allocation amount of the fixed overhead cost to inventory is 120 million yen $(1,000 \div (9,000 + 1,000) \times 1,200 = 120)$. If overproduction leads to 3,000 units, the allocation amount is 300 million yen $(3,000 \div (9,000 + 3,000) \times 1,200 = 300)$. *Ceteris paribus,* the cost of inventory increases by 180 million yen. The net income also increases by the same amount.

We can exhibit many traditional manipulations on inventory that are not illegal but are highly strategic or intentional, such as the manipulation of the quality standard of a product, changing the accounting valuation procedure from FIFO to LIFO under an inflation period of time, and so on.

Managers can also decrease their profit from adverse manipulations such as from slim production, applying strict quality standards, changing from LIFO to FIFO, and so on. We find such relationships between earnings and inventory that an inventory increase usually leads to an earnings increase and, usually, an inventory decrease results in an earnings decrease. It is assumed that inventory change may be utilized as a typical component of income smoothing.

On the other hand, the just-in-time (JIT) system that is part of the Toyota Production System requires "order-driven-production." Then, the JIT system has a check mechanism for restraining income smoothing by inventory change.

Do managers have an incentive to use this relationship for income smoothing even under the JIT system in the Japanese automobile industry? The purpose of my research is to answer this question.

2 Discretionary Models and Hypotheses

2.1 *Discretionary accruals: the modified DJ model*

Healy (1985) defined accruals as the difference between net income and cash flow from operations, as follows:

$$\text{Total Accruals } (TA) = \text{Net Income } (NI) \\ - \text{Cash Flow from Operation } (CFO) \quad (1)$$

Healy defined discretionary accruals as total accruals minus non-discretionary accruals that are a normal part of accruals reflecting working capital circulation, as follows:

$$\text{Discretionary Accruals } (DA) \\ = \text{Total Accruals } (TA) - \text{Non-discretionary Accruals } (NDA) \quad (2)$$

However, what is called the normal part of accruals is not clear. Healy applied the average value of five years of accruals, while DeAngelo (1986) used accruals from the last year. Jones (1991) regressed accruals on sales. In this study, I use the new data of cash flow from operations only applicable for eight years. I have to avoid data loss from estimating the normal discretionary part and I choose to adopt DeAngelo's assumption. Next, I assume that accruals change proportionally to sales. This assumption is a simple application of Jones, and thus I call my discretionary accruals model the modified DJ model.

Discretionary accruals: the modified DJ model

$$DA_t/S_t = TA_t/S_t - TA_{t-1}/S_{t-1} \tag{3}$$

2.2 *Discretionary day's inventory*

This paper focuses on the day's inventory (= inventory ÷ sales × 365) when examining the relationships between the introduction of the JIT system and income smoothing behavior by managers. Changes in the discretionary day's inventory ($D\Delta INV_t/S_t$) may be a main component of discretionary accruals. The day's inventory change ($\Delta INV_t/S_t$) is a negative component of cash flow from operations in cash flow statements, and cash flow from operation is a negative component of accruals (Equation 1). In this case, the relationship between accruals and the day's inventory change is positive. The positive relationship may introduce a change in the discretionary day's inventory in Equation 4 from the discretionary accruals of Equation 3, as follows:

Discretionary day's inventory change: the modified DJ/S model

$$D\Delta INV_t/S_t = \Delta INV_t/S_t - \Delta INV_{t-1}/S_{t-1} \tag{4}$$

Strictly speaking, a more exact relationship exists between the day's inventory and the cost of goods sold. I also define the discretionary day's inventory (= inventory ÷ cost of goods sold × 365) as a main component of accruals, as follows:

Discretionary day's inventory change: the modified DJ/C model

$$D\Delta INV_t/C_t = \Delta INV_t/C_t - \Delta INV_{t-1}/C_{t-1} \tag{5}$$

We cannot identify prior earnings before earnings management and it is difficult to classify a firm-year as an income increasing firm-year or an income decreasing firm-year by using post earnings after earnings management. I focus on the cash flow from operations, which is sometimes called hard profit. I introduce the following assumptions and hypotheses.

3   Assumptions and Hypotheses

3.1 *Assumptions*

A firm-year with an earnings increase before potential earnings management is assumed to have positive ΔCFO.

A firm-year with an earnings decrease before potential earnings management is assumed to have negative ΔCFO.

3.2 *Hypothesis 1: discretionary accruals (DA/S)*

A firm-year makes income smooth by using discretionary accruals.

Type A: *conservative accounting*
Positive ΔCFO leads to negative discretionary accruals (DA/S).
Type B: *window dressing*
Negative ΔCFO leads to positive discretionary accruals (DA/S).

3.2.1 *Null hypothesis 1*

H1. There is no difference in mean values of discretionary accruals (DA/S) between the positive ΔCFO Group and negative ΔCFO Group.

3.3 *Hypothesis 2: discretionary day's inventory change (DΔINV/S or DΔINV/C)*

A firm-year makes income smooth by using the discretionary day's inventory change.

Type A: *conservative accounting*
Positive ΔCFO leads to a negative discretionary day's inventory change
    ($D\Delta$INV/S or DΔINV/C).

Type B: window dressing

Negative ΔCFO leads to a positive discretionary day's inventory change

(DΔINV/S or DΔINV/C).

3.3.1 Null hypothesis 2

H2S. There is no difference in mean values of the discretionary day's inventory change (DΔINV/S) between the positive ΔCFO Group and negative ΔCFO Group.

H2C. There is no difference in mean values of the discretionary day's inventory change (DΔINV/C) between the positive ΔCFO Group and negative ΔCFO Group.

I divide the firm-years sample into two groups for testing my two hypotheses. I call the positive firm-year group with a positive increment of cash flow from operations the positive ΔCFO Group and the negative firm-year group with a negative increment of cash flow from operations the negative ΔCFO Group.

The above null hypothesis does not directly test the income smoothing hypothesis, but it does test a symptom of the income smoothing by using the discretionary day's inventory change. Here, I dismiss the problem of errors in variables on cash flow from operations by using sales (or cost of goods sold) deflating CFO as the explanatory variables for testing the null hypotheses.

4 Data and Day's Inventory

4.1 Data

I sample all 57 firms of the Japanese automobile industry listed on the first section of the Tokyo Stock Exchange from fiscal year December 2000 to December 2007 in the Nikkei Needs Database. I classify these 57 firms into 26 firms of the Toyota group and 31 firms of other groups based on both capital-holdings and sales-production relationships. I can use only eight fiscal years' data after the accounting big bang in 1999, since we can use cash flow from operations in the cash flow statements. I have samples of 399 firm-years (57 firms $\times$ 7 years), because the first-year data of cash flow from operations is utilized for the difference calculation.

4.2 Day's inventory: descriptive statistics

Figure 1 shows the day's inventory (inventory/sales × 365) of 399 firm-years in the Japanese automobile industry from fiscal year 2000 to 2006. In this period, the industry enjoyed aggressive direct investment in foreign countries with the gradual growth of overseas sales and profit.

The average value of a day's inventory in the parent company is 16.25 days and the median is 13.65 days. These days nearly correspond to the period from the customer order to delivery to the customer in domestic sales. The average value of a day's inventory in consolidated financial statements is 26.41 days and the median is 25.02 days. These periods may approximately correspond to above two weeks and another 10 days that may be necessary for shipping finished cars and their parts by balloon ships or other cargo ships. In particular, the average days of a day's finished goods and a day's raw materials are high and they show, respectively, 11.48 days and 8.23 days in consolidated financial statements, mainly because of the shipping period.

5 Results

5.1 Comparison of the positive △CFO Group with the negative △CFO Group in the discretionary accruals

I will examine the following null hypothesis in this section H1. There is no difference in mean values of discretionary accruals (DA/S) between the positive ΔCFO Group and negative ΔCFO Group.

Figure 2 exhibits a clear difference of the positive ΔCFO Group with the negative ΔCFO Group in mean values of discretionary accruals (DA/S) on the total sample, Toyota group, and other groups. Positive ΔCFO may lead to negative discretionary accruals (DA/S) under conservative accounting. Negative ΔCFO may lead to positive discretionary accruals (DA/S) under window dressing accounting.

a. Total sample	Consolidated			(days)
	Inventory	Finished goods	Work in process	Raw materials
Firm-year	399	178	170	171
Mean	26.409	11.476	6.870	8.233
Median	25.019	8.547	6.142	6.812
Mini	3.101	0.014	0.810	1.388
Max	81.172	46.575	22.989	27.150

b. Toyota group	Consolidated			(days)
	Inventory	Finished goods	Work in process	Raw materials
Firm-year	182	92	91	92
Mean	25.622	11.398	7.587	6.311
Median	23.359	10.266	6.282	5.695
Mini	3.782	0.149	0.810	1.442
Max	81.172	32.038	22.989	16.256

c. Other group	Consolidated			(days)
	Inventory	Finished goods	Work in process	Raw materials
Firm-year	217	86	79	79
Mean	27.069	11.560	6.043	10.470
Median	26.796	7.078	5.875	9.424
Mini	3.101	0.014	0.980	1.388
Max	65.548	46.575	14.653	27.150

d. Difference test in Means between Toyota and Other groups... Consolidated				
	Inventory	Finished goods	Work in process	Raw materials
t value	−1.072	−0.107	2.410	−5.003
p value	0.142	0.457	0.009	0.000001

e. Total sample	Parent company			(days)
	Inventory	Finished goods	Work in process	Raw materials
Firm-year	399	399	399	399
Mean	16.247	5.193	7.241	3.812
Median	13.640	4.337	5.109	2.929
Mini	2.369	0.000	0.166	0.094
Max	77.905	21.717	77.777	17.553

Note: day's inventory = inventory/sales ∗ 365.
Source: Fiscal year December 2000 to December 2007, data from Nikkei Needs.

Fig. 1   Day's inventory in Japanese automobile industry.

	Positive ΔCFO	Negative ΔCFO	t value	p value
	day	day		
Total sample	−6.296	4.617	−7.448	0.000
Toyota group	−7.132	5.811	−7.005	0.000
Other group	−5.555	3.697	−4.207	0.000

Assumption: A firm-year with earnings increase (decrease) before potential earnings management is assumed to have positive (negative) ΔCFO.
Hypothesis: H1. Positive (negative) ΔCFO leads to negative (positive) discretionary accruals.
Modified DJ model: $DA/S = (TA_t/S_t - TA_{t-1}/S_{t-1})$.
Where: DA: discretionary accruals, TA: total accruals, S: sales, Δ: difference.
Sample: from fiscal year December 2000 to December 2007 in the Japanese automobile industry with 57 firms, 399 firm-years.

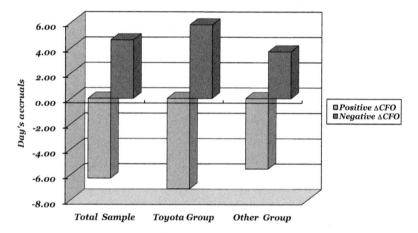

Fig. 2   Discretionary accruals (DA) of positive ΔCFO and negative ΔCFO comparing the Toyota group and other groups.

In the case of the total sample, Fig. 2 shows the negative 6.30 days in positive ΔCFO and positive 4.62 days in negative ΔCFO. The high t value more than two and the low p value less than one percent in Fig. 2 tell us that H1 is rejected at the one-percent significance level. In that case, it is assumed that discretionary accruals may make use of possible income smoothing.

Positive ΔCFO results in negative 7.13 days of discretionary accruals (DA/S) and negative ΔCFO results in positive 5.81 days of discretionary accruals (DA/S) in the Toyota group. Positive ΔCFO results in negative 5.56 days of discretionary accruals (DA/S) and negative ΔCFO results in positive 3.70 days of discretionary accruals (DA/S) on other groups. I find no clear difference between the Toyota group and other groups. The concept of discretionary accruals has a strong power for detecting earnings management, but it is artificial for improving the business cycle. Next, I apply this concept to the day's inventory.

5.2 Comparison of the positive ΔCFO Group with the negative ΔCFO Group in the discretionary day's inventory change based on sales

In this section, I will test the null hypothesis H2S. There is no difference in mean values of the discretionary day's inventory change (DΔINV/S) between the positive ΔCFO Group and negative ΔCFO Group.

Figure 3 shows the difference of positive ΔCFO Group with negative ΔCFO Group in mean values of the discretionary day's inventory change (DΔINV/S) on the total sample, the Toyota group, and other groups. In the case of the total sample, Fig. 3 shows the negative 0.05 days in positive ΔCFO and positive 1.27 days in negative ΔCFO. The t value more than two and the low p value less than one percent in Fig. 3 tell us that the H2S is rejected at the one-percent significance level. In this case, it is assumed that discretionary accruals may make use of possible income smoothing.

In the Toyota group, positive ΔCFO results in positive (not negative) 0.04 days of the discretionary day's inventory change (DΔINV/S) and negative ΔCFO results in positive 0.71 days of the discretionary day's inventory change (DΔINV/S). On other groups, positive ΔCFO results in negative 0.12 days of discretionary accruals (DA/S) and negative ΔCFO results in positive 1.70 days of the discretionary day's inventory change (DΔINV/S). The comparison of the Toyota group with other groups shows a different sign of discretionary day's inventory change (DΔINV/S). The Toyota group in positive ΔCFO is not negative but is positive 0.04 days. Positive ΔCFO does not lead to a negative discretionary day's inventory

$\Delta\Delta$NV/S	Positive ΔCFO	Negative ΔCFO	t value	p value
	day	day		
Inventory				
Total sample	−0.045	1.272	−3.285	0.001
Toyota group	0.035	0.709	−1.374	0.086
Other group	−0.116	1.704	−3.026	0.002
Finished goods				
Total sample	−0.161	0.644	−2.074	0.020
Toyota group	0.000	−0.087	0.180	0.429
Other group	−0.351	1.284	−2.777	0.004
Work in process				
Total sample	−0.219	0.324	−2.499	0.007
Toyota group	−0.237	0.009	−1.125	0.132
Other group	−0.195	0.618	−2.224	0.015
Raw material				
Total sample	0.162	0.628	−1.916	0.029
Toyota group	0.166	0.228	−0.268	0.395
Other group	0.158	1.001	−2.104	0.019

Assumption: A firm-year with earnings increase (decrease) before potential earnings management is assumed to have positive (negative) ΔCFO.
Hypothesis: H2S. Positive (negative) ΔCFO leads to negative (positive) DΔINV/S.
Modified DJ-S model: DΔINV/S = (ΔINV$_t$/S$_t$ − ΔINV$_{t-1}$/S$_{t-1}$) ∗ 365.
Where: INV: inventory, S: sales, Δ: difference.
Sample: from fiscal year December 2000 to December 2007 in the Japanese automobile industry with 57 firms, 399 firm-years (Toyota Group 247, Other Group 152).
Fig. 3   Discretionary day's inventory change (DΔINV/S) of positive ΔCFO and negative ΔCFO comparing the Toyota group and other groups.

change (DΔINV/S) in the Toyota group. The t value of 1.37 and the p value of 0.09 in Fig. 4 tell us that the H2S is rejected at the ten-percent significance level. In this case, the discretionary day's inventory change (DΔINV/S) might be used for possible income smoothing. I find a clear difference between the Toyota group and other groups.

Additionally, I will test the null hypothesis H2S1 (H2S2, H2S3). There is no difference in mean values of the discretionary day's finished goods (or work in process or raw materials) and change between the positive ΔCFO Group and the negative ΔCFO Group.

The above difference is clearer in the case of the components of inventory, that is, finished goods, work in process, and raw materials. Figure 3 rejects these null hypotheses at the ten-percent significance

$\Delta\Delta INV/S$	Positive ΔCFO	Negative ΔCFO	t value	p value
	day	day		
Inventory				
Total sample	0.097	1.330	−2.562	0.005
Toyota group	0.104	0.680	−0.922	0.179
Other group	0.090	1.829	−2.472	0.007
Finished goods				
Total sample	−0.164	0.724	−1.851	0.034
Toyota group	0.016	−0.164	0.303	0.381
Other group	−0.377	1.501	−2.600	0.006
Work in process				
Total sample	−0.217	0.303	−2.079	0.020
Toyota group	−0.253	−0.053	−0.755	0.226
Other group	−0.172	0.635	−1.976	0.026
Raw material				
Total sample	0.239	0.686	−1.564	0.061
Toyota group	0.205	0.226	−0.077	0.469
Other group	0.284	1.114	−1.753	0.042

Assumption: A firm-year with earnings increase (decrease) before potential earnings management is assumed to have positive (negative) ΔCFO.
Hypothesis: H2C. Positive (negative) ΔCFO leads to negative (positive) $D\Delta INV/C$.
Modified DJ-C model: $D\Delta INV/C = (\Delta INV_t/C_t - \Delta INV_{t-1}/C_{t-1}) * 365$.
Where: INV: inventory, C: cost of goods sold, Δ: difference
Sample: from fiscal year December 2000 to December 2007 in the Japanese automobile industry with 57 firms, 399 firm-years (Toyota Group 247, Other Group 152).

Fig. 4 Discretionary day's inventory change ($D\Delta INV/C$) of positive ΔCFO and negative ΔCFO comparing the Toyota group and other groups.

level for finished goods (t value is positive), work in process (p value is 0.13), and raw materials (p value is 0.39) in the Toyota group and they show clear evidence of income smoothing by finished goods, work in process, and raw materials on other groups.

5.3 Comparison of a positive ΔCFO Group with a negative ΔCFO Group in the discretionary day's inventory change based on cost of goods sold

This section will show the result of testing the null hypothesis H2C. There is no difference in mean values of the discretionary day's inventory change ($D\Delta INV/C$) between the positive ΔCFO Group and negative ΔCFO Group.

In the case of the total sample, Fig. 4 shows the positive (not negative) 0.10 days in the positive ΔCFO and positive 1.33 days in the negative ΔCFO. The t value more than two and the low p value less than one percent in Fig. 4 tell us that the H2C is rejected at the one-percent significance level.

Positive ΔCFO results in positive (not negative) 0.10 days of the discretionary day's inventory change (DΔINV/S) and negative ΔCFO results in positive 0.68 days of the discretionary day's inventory change (DΔINV/S) in the Toyota group. Positive ΔCFO results in positive (not negative) 0.09 days of discretionary accruals (DA/S) and negative ΔCFO results in positive 1.83 days of the discretionary day's inventory change (DΔINV/C) in other groups. The t value of 0.92 and the p value of 0.18 in Fig. 4 tell us that the H2C is not rejected at the ten-percent significance level.

Additionally, I will test the null hypothesis H2C1 (H2C2, H2C3). There is no difference in mean values of the discretionary day's finished goods (or work in process or raw materials) change between the positive ΔCFO Group and negative ΔCFO Group components of inventory, that is, finished goods, work in process, and raw materials.

Figure 4 does not reject the null hypotheses at the ten-percent significance level for finished goods (t value is positive), work in process (p value is 0.23), and raw materials (p value is 0.47) in the Toyota group. On the contrary, Fig. 4 shows clear evidence of income smoothing by finished goods, work in process, and raw materials in other groups.

6 Conclusion

I examine the income smoothing behavior based on inventory in the Japanese automobile industry based on seven years of recent financial data. I identify the symptom of income smoothing behavior by possible handling of the day's inventory, excluding the Toyota group. The discretionary day's inventory is explained by income smoothing behavior of managers in groups other than the Toyota group.

Generally speaking, in the less profitable period of time with negative ΔCFO, the day's inventory (inventory/sales $\times$ 365) may increase because of the inventory increase and sales decrease, and in contrast, in the more profitable period with positive ΔCFO, the day's inventory may decrease because of the inventory decrease and sales increase. This relationship can be said as the automatic earnings stabilizing system under the over-production hypothesis. I find that the JIT System of the Toyota group under order-driven TPS is more powerful than the stabilizing system. Next, I want to answer the question of why the Toyota group shows stronger prevailing power against income smoothing than other groups under what appears to be the same JIT System.

Acknowledgment

This paper is based on the valuable discussions among members of the Toyota Project on Meijo Process Management. I appreciate the valuable comments of Makoto Kawada, Toshiharu Nakane, Toshio Ohashi, Noriyuki Imai, Masatomo Tanaka, and Tohru Niwa. This project was supported by the 2007 research program (C) (No. 17530349) and by the 2008 research program (B) (No. 20330096) of the Ministry of Education and Science and by the 2007 Strategic Research Program funded by Meijo University. I am grateful for the assistance with data processing by Mitsuru Kubo.

References

DeAngelo, L (1986). Accounting numbers as market valuation substitute. *Accounting Review*, 61, 400–420.
Healy, PM (1985). The effect of bonus schemes on accounting decisions. *Journal of Accounting and Economics*, 7, 85–107.
Jones, J (1991). Earnings management during import relief investigations. *Journal of Accounting Research*, 29, 193–228.
Roychowdhury, S (2006). Earnings management through real activities manipulation. *Journal of Accounting and Economics*, 42, 335–370.

5

M&A and Its Incentive System for the Inter-Firm Organization

Yasuhiro Monden
Professor of Mejiro University
Professor Emeritus of Tsukuba University

1 Research Purpose

I believe that the design or reorganization of a corporate organization should be discussed from the perspective of the supply-and-demand equilibrium in the market. In reality, bankruptcies of individual companies due to overproduction or lack of demand and imbalance between supply and demand in the industry always occur, and, in Japan, recession lasted for more than 10 years starting from the 1990s. Although the tendency of attaching great importance to the stock market is not challenged in merger-and-acquisition (M&A) business circles and in the so-called global standards, in some cases, the stock market goes out of control because it is a speculative market. In Japan, the economic bubble reached a peak by the beginning of the 1990s, after which the bubble suddenly collapsed. The collapse of the bubble set off a recession that lasted as long as 15 years.

As just described, it is quite difficult to balance supply and demand by relying on the price mechanism of the market.

It is my position that the supply-and-demand equilibrium should be attained by means of an organization. As an antithesis to today's predominance of market fundamentalism espoused by economists from Adam Smith to Hayek and Milton Friedman, I would like to propose a new institutional fundamentalism keeping the merits of market competition. An essential matter is that the mechanism of synchronizing the product supply from one's own company with the changes in demand in the market should be incorporated in this "organization."

My initial idea therefore *was* the creation of a "vertically integrated organization" in a company, encompassing all areas from research and development to production and sales, with the aim of shortening the distance between the upstream supply and the personnel in charge of satisfying demand, who are near to the downstream end users, thus balancing the supply and demand. However, such a vertically integrated organization created within a company would inevitably become large-scale, and if supply is cut at the time of scarcity of demand, the company cannot recover the fixed cost; that is, it would be quite difficult for the company to generate profits.

Therefore, a vertically allied organization (inter-firm network) that makes it possible to adjust supply and demand while securing profitability in each commodities market instead of the above vertically integrated organization is advisable. In this paper, I discuss ways to design such an organization from the viewpoint of M&A and then clarify how to control or motivate the member companies of the network through an incentive system called an incentive price.

2   What is the Network Organization?

What I think as a good organization is some vertically *allied* organization. Such organization is so-called "network organization" or "virtual organization."

The network organization stands for the structure of organization that allies with other companies who have some competitive functional merit in the markets, keeping the self-function of their own that has core competence among various functions of R&D, manufacturing, distribution, sales, and so forth. This is different from utilizing the outsourcing from independent company on the market base, but it is a series of alliances (including the "Keiretsu") among vertical functional firms. Thus, this network can be called a supply-chain or the inter-firm relations.

For making such alliances, the top management of any company should ask themselves about "what is a raison d'etre or existence value for their company." In other words, they have to recognize "what their company can contribute to the society and what competence they have for their selling to the customers compared to other companies in the business world."

Ever since the knowledge and expertise necessary for business activities have become advanced and specialized, it has become more difficult for single companies to cover all the functional areas or train intellectual employees. Therefore, it has become easier for a network organization than for a vertically *integrated* organization consisting of a single company to keep abreast of the latest state-of-the-art technology and maintain a highly advanced level of expertise in multiple functional areas.

The network or alliance in this context implies the long-term relations of transactions that include technological alliance, joint development, mutual licensing, joint manufacturing, production consignment (production on commission), sales consignment (sales on commission), capital alliance, joint venture, and moreover include establishment of affiliated company and merger. The important point that I recommend here is not to establish any vertically *integrated single* company, but to construct some inter-firm network.

Let us define the network organization again. It is a network that multiple firms will construct, but it behaves as if it is a single company with mutual cooperation among constructing companies. The network usually consists of a core company and many other companies who will obey the instructions of the central right of the core company. The central company will take part of only its outstanding functional field and it will outsource all other functional areas where each of them has its own competence.

2.1 *Boundaries of the inter-firm network as an open adaptive system*

Once Cyert and March (1963) has recognized the business organization as an adaptive system to the external environment, which would determine the decision factors (endogenous variables) responding to the external environmental factors (exogenous variables). Such adaptive system is grasped in a stimulus-and-reaction relationship. A network organization is also one of such open adaptive system.

The network organization will withdraw from the unprofitable business whose demand has declined and catch the other independent company that has some desirable new business. Therefore, the network organization is not a fixed formation of allied firms, but its members will depart from and enter the network in question intermittently when time goes by. Thus, the boundaries of the inter-firm network are fuzzy and there exists no hard wall between the external market and internal organization.

Suppose, for instance, that a core company of a network organization is the holding company and it catches a certain company existing outside the network by applying the stock exchange, as a 100%-owned affiliated company. Then, since both of these companies remain as legally independent companies, it can be said that they formed a new network or they merged essentially.

3 The Concept that Makes the Network Organization Unique

Let me try to propose a *core concept of the network organization*. The proper feature of network organization is that this organization can make new *value-creation* through joint activities of participating companies. Further the decision of participation in this organization by the participants, who are independent companies, will be made considering if the incentives given by the core company to each participant could be satisfied by each participant.

Such incentives are the allocated amount of the anticipated "additional values" created by the joint cooperative works after participation. Such additional value, created value, or premium value is equivalent to the so-called "synergy effect," which is also called "*complementarities*."

Such nature exists neither in the pure market nor in the pure organization. That is, neither in the pure market nor in the pure organization the concept of incremental value through cooperative activities of multiple independent companies does exist. Only the value created by the independent activities of a single company (that is "standalone value" created by a single company) does exist. Therefore, the readers can easily understand that the above characteristics of network organization were not derived from any nature of both the *pure market* and the *pure* organization.[1]

If we consider the relationship between the synergy effect concept and the Course's transaction cost concept, the "transaction cost saved" when the transaction was conducted within the internal organization is made is merely a portion of the synergy effect. That is, the former is a partial set of the latter. The synergy effect by the inter-firm cooperation includes not only the saved transaction cost, but also the following effects:

- Restructure effect of redundant functions appeared in a combined company;
- Cost reduction effect through the economy of scale;
- The increased sales through joint utilization of each other's sales channels;
- Combination of technologies; and
- Increase sales revenues and profits caused by the new products developed through combination of technologies, and so forth.

4   Three Roles of the Core Company in a Network Organization

Since a network organization is a "network of various companies," the presence of a core company that plays the role of headquarters is essential. Although the actions of the companies participating in the network are under the control of the centralized power of the core company; some power is granted to the participating companies for their decentralized decisions within the network, just as in vertically integrated companies under the multi-divisional system.[2]

The roles played by the core company of a network organization are the following three[3]:

1. Recognition of the functions (roles) to be shared among the companies participating in the network and the selection of the member companies. This is the *strategic decision No. 1.*

The *strategic decision No.* 2 that the core company should undertake is to determine the forms of business combination of inter-firm relations.

2. One more role is to encourage candidate member companies to participate in the network. In order to make the participation in the network appear attractive to the candidate member companies, the core company decides the share of the profits as an incentive and it presents the proposal to the candidate companies. This role is one of *"management control"* functions of the core company.

However, the core company cannot force the candidate member companies to become members of the network, because even if the core company tries to force a candidate company to become a member by attempting a hostile acquisition by capital strength or launching a hostile takeover bid (TOB), the candidate company can defend itself by seeking the help of other companies outside the network or by introducing the poison pill.

3. Determination of the allocation of resources among the companies participating in the network or determination of the adjustment of supply and demand.

A network usually consists of member companies from the upstream to the downstream levels of a supply chain and the core company determines the quantitative allocation of goods in supply and demand among the member companies. That is, in response to the fluctuations in supply and demand in the market, the adjustment of supply and demand of the product relevant to the supply chain is made quickly throughout the chain under the direct quantitative control of the core company. This role is usually mechanically conducted by applying the MRP (Material Resource Planning) system imbedded in the basic operational software of ERP, and it is called *"task control* or *operational control."*

Furthermore, since individual companies do not have a great amount of fixed assets, they can adapt themselves flexibly to the situation and attain their own supply-and-demand equilibrium through the network relatively easily. Since each company has a relatively small amount of fixed assets, they incur a relatively small fixed cost, including depreciation and amortization costs, so they can carry out production adjustment relatively easily.

5 Strategic Decision No. 1: Selection of Network Participating Companies Through M&A

The reason why M&A is increasing in Japan is that since new technologies are emerging enormously in the industrial world, people wish to introduce such technologies into their companies and thereby evoke the seeds of new demand and create many new demands.

Mr. Kotaro Higuchi, emeritus chairperson of Asahi Beer Company, said as follows (2000):

"Although only the excess supply due to the over-capacity and over-employment is emphasized under the current recession of the "lost ten years," the essential problem does not lie in such points but lies in whether or not we can quickly change ourselves in order to concentrate the managerial resources on the business fields where the customer's wants and needs exist. For this purpose the research and development that meet market are the most critical."

However, it takes longer time to develop such technologies by the single company. Thus in order to "buy the time" necessary for developing such technologies and linking them to attractive products for the customer, the companies are making joint venture, affiliated company, merger, capital alliance, and so forth, so that technical innovation can be made and it creates some new demand.

In the merger of Konica and Minoruta conducted in August 2003, it was expected that Konica's toner technology and Minoruta's color-print technology would create synergy effect so that some new color toner would be developed. This is an action to create a new demand in the market.

On the other hand, they are restructuring the production capacities such as plants, facilities, and human resources by integrating them through M&A of the two companies in the same industries, which is called a horizontal integration. This is a reduction of supply capacity. In the above merger of Konica and Minoruta, their initial short-run and direct synergy effect was cost reductions due to the scale merit. There are reduction in the number of locations by integrating both companies manufacturing plants, reduction of labor costs (4800 people were reduced), cost savings due to merchandize integration, and so forth. Also they make withdrawal from the less profitable business domains that became obsolete.

As such, increase or decrease of business scale through M&A implies that the firm is dynamically adapting to the fluctuations in supply and demand in the market. The network organization does such adaptive behavior as an open adaptive system.

6   Strategic Decision No. 2: Design of Forms of the Inter-Firm Combination

There are various types of inter-firm combination in a network organization, which lie between the full market transactions advocated by Adam Smith and the fully vertically integrated organizations seen until the 1920s (such as Standard Oil, US Steel, and so forth) examined by A. Chandler (1977). Figure 1 below shows the types of inter-firm combination arranged in order of the degree of combination (or the degree of interdependence).

Types of combination	Control power	Synergy effect	Risk of fixed-cost recovery failure
Merger	Maximum	Maximum	Maximum
Affiliated company			
Capital alliance			
Operational alliance	Minimum	Minimum	Minimum
Market transactions	0	0	0

Fig. 1   The types of inter-firm combination.

Inter-firm Supply Chain

Supply chain of operational alliance	Supply chain of capital alliance			Supply chain of consolidated business group		Member changes by merger, acquisition, and buying the split-off business in the supply chain	
	Minor stock holding	Mutual stock holding	Joint venture	Stock holding of over 20%	Stock holding of over 50% by stock acquisition or TOB	100% affiliated company by stock exchange	Holding company by stock transfer
Technological alliance, joint development, mutual licensing, joint manufacturing, production consignment, sales consignment	Long-term alliance of transactions		Combination by mutual business split-off. Withdrawal from un-profitable business	Influencing on the related company	Governance on the affiliated company	Governance through acquisition of new business company	

Fig. 2   Purpose and techniques of forming the various types of networks.

The types of inter-firm combination, from full market transactions through operational alliance and capital alliance to integration into a company as an affiliated company and merger, shown at the left end of Fig. 1, can be selectively adopted or jointly used by the core company for the participating companies in a network.

The purpose and techniques of the operational alliance, capital alliance, affiliated company, and merger in Fig. 1 are summarized in Fig. 2. Note that the author assumes the inter-firm network as a supply chain.

6.1 *Merger*

6.1.1 *Acquisition price as incentive to M&A*

In Fig. 2, the merger is a complete enterprise integration, so the independence of the company merged into another company as a legal entity is lost, but the fact that such a strong type of inter-firm combination is adopted in some cases within a network poses no problem. When a merger or capital alliance is carried out between existing member companies in a network, it means that "transactions motivated by a *price incentive* within the network organization through M&A" are made inside the organization.

That is, in the case where two companies that have been independent in terms of capital in a network form a capital alliance as minority stockholders, the amount of the stock acquisition price in the TOB (or tender offer) will become the *price incentive* for the stockholders of the target company to be acquired by the other company. Also, in the case where the two companies fully merge, the amount of the acquisition price of the merged company becomes the price incentive. These are carried out as transactions in the network organization, not as market transactions. This incentive is the allocation of the so-called "synergy effect" of the merger in question.

6.1.2 *Control right: origin of synergy effect*

Among the types of inter-firm combination in a network organization, the maximum synergy effect can be obtained when the integrator takes control of the target company, because the integrator can restructure the target company at its own discretion. This is the merit of a vertically integrated company. Unless the integrator takes control of the target company, the restructuring of the target company cannot always be carried out resolutely, because the target company is managed by the management thereof as before. In the case of inter-firm combinations that are looser than a merger, such as capital alliance by minority stockholders, the synergy effect is less pronounced than in the case where full control of the target company is taken, even if there is a certain synergy effect.[4]

Then, what would be the reason for the creation of a network organization instead of a merger, which has the maximum synergy effect? The answer lies in the demerits of a vertically integrated organization. However, the increase in the adjustment cost, coordination cost, or management cost pointed out by orthodox organizational economists, including Coase (1937), and so forth, as a demerit is practically negligible thanks to the progress in information technology (IT) such as intra-net, EDI, and so forth. Rather, the author considers the following demerits as problematic:

1. Risk of fixed-cost recovery failure

As I have repeatedly mentioned, this is a disadvantage of an organization consisting of a single company; that is, since the single integrated company should possess enormous fixed assets on its own, it incurs a high risk of fixed-cost recovery failure. The network organization can spread this risk among the member companies.

2. Difficulty in allocating profit in a mutually satisfactory manner

As Adam Smith also stressed, a company cannot be the best of all companies in all areas. This was the reason why Smith advocated both the division of labor among companies and market transactions according to prices. However, the market pricing system is not always conducive to a balance between supply and demand. Here, the network organization solves the problem. Each company participates in the network in the area where it has an advantage over others and it goes into partnership with others in other areas. It deserves special emphasis that Smith advocated "market transactions," whereas I advocate "transactions within a network organization," which are different from market transactions.

Then, why are the companies, each of which has a core competence in an area, not fully integrated into a new company? In my opinion, they are not fully integrated into a new company because the profit obtainable from the maintenance of independence may be greater than that obtainable from the formation of a *total coalition*.[5]

6.2 *Placing a company under control as an affiliate*

The integrator places a company participating in the network under control as an affiliate by acquiring the majority of the voting stock of that company. Its main aim is to receive the benefits of the "synergy effect" referred to in Section 6.1.

In my opinion, regarding the degree of vertical combination of companies in a network organization, the state of the parent company and its 100%-owned affiliates in terms of capital is not always the best, because the result of such integration is equivalent to a single company in terms of capital. That is, such integration will make it difficult to swiftly respond to the change in demand of the relevant product in the market, because the assets and liabilities of all the companies participating in the network appear *fully* on the consolidated balance sheet of the integrator; thus, the integrator or the company leading the consolidated business group should bear all the fixed assets and it should take the risk of fixed-cost recovery failure as a single company, as in the case of a merger.

However, it would be desirable for the companies participating in a network to form a capital alliance in order to establish relations between the integrator and its consolidate subsidiaries that are not wholly owned by the parent company or relations between the integrator and its "equity-method" applied affiliates. Although consolidated accounts are created even in this case, the amount of fixed assets to be borne by the whole consolidated business group is lessened compared to that to be borne by a practical single company consisting of the above parent company and its 100%-owned subsidiaries. This makes it easier to respond to market fluctuations.

The role of stockholders in society is to supply capital to companies and assume the risk for the results of business operations. By having so-called minor stockholders for each company in the stock market outside the network organization instead of establishing a relationship between the parent company and its 100%-owned subsidiaries in the network organization, the network organization as a business group can allot the risk of loss to both the parent company and the minor stockholders. Because while in consolidated accounts the total assets of the subsidiaries are recorded on the balance sheet of the parent company, the *amount attributable to minor stockholders of the losses* incurred by the subsidiaries due to their production cuts are deducted from the consolidated loss in the consolidated profit and loss account. The top executives of the relevant subsidiaries should share the responsibility for the losses incurred by the minor stockholders.

6.3 *Capital alliance*

There are three types of capital alliance: 1. *participation as a minor stockholder*, 2. *mutual holdings of stocks*, and 3. *joint venture*; the degree of alliance becomes stronger in this order.

First, even if the capital participation is in the form of minor stockholders, the right to participate in management as a stockholder is secured, so some synergy effect can be expected. However, from the position of a minor stockholder, it is impossible to get involved deeply in the business projects of the company upon specifying the use of the invested capital, so the degree of involvement is limited.

Today, the main purpose of *"mutual holdings of stocks"* is the protection of companies against hostile takeovers.

As for joint ventures, usually the equity position is equal. Now that the form of investment is a joint venture for a specific business project, the target for which the invested money is used is limited. That is, each investor can exercise its right to participate in the joint

venture within the limit of its capital investment, and the risk and
return can be shared among the investors. However, since a joint
venture is based on the principle of equal capital investment, any
company that has a stake therein cannot take control of the joint venture. Then, what is the concrete form of a joint venture in a network
organization? This is, for example, the case where two subsidiaries
in a consolidated business group or two companies that form a capital alliance split off the same kind of business from their respective
business operations, and transfer them to a newly established joint
venture. (In the business combination accounting standard in Japan,
this is called the "formation of jointly controlled transactions.")

Next let us see a case of the *participation as a minor stockholder.*
Toyota Motors has stakes in parts manufacturers under its control
merely as a minor stockholder, but Toyota practically controls them.
Regarding Toyota's relationship with major parts manufacturers,
since most of their products are for Toyota, Toyota is the core company of the group of parts companies (network organization). Also,
since Toyota's major parts manufacturers have directors dispatched
from Toyota, their decisions regarding supply quantities are made
according to Toyota's instructions.

Nevertheless, the parts manufacturers for Toyota (such as Denso,
Aisin, and Toyoda Gosei) also supply parts to finished-car manufacturers other than Toyota. This makes it possible for the parts
manufacturers to spread the risk of any drop in demand for Toyota
parts. These parts manufacturers can consider themselves as the core
companies (integrators) of their respective networks, which include
their multiple customers.

6.4   *Business tie-up (operational alliance)*

A business tie-up or an operational alliance is mainly a long-term (a
few years) agreement on outsourcing in a supply chain. It signifies the
establishment of cooperative relations between companies concerning
a specific functional operation, such as development, manufacturing,
sales, information processing, or general administration (personnel
affairs, legal affairs, accounting, and so forth). However, there are also

cases where companies of the same trade enter into a cross-licensing agreement for patented technology in order to cooperate in the development of new products.

In the case where companies participating in a network only have a business tie-up without equity participation, consolidated accounting does not apply to these companies; instead, only single accounts for the individual companies are maintained. Therefore, the business results of individual companies are evaluated by the stock market. In this case, since the outcome of the management of the network group as a whole is not evaluated by the stock market, the risk involved in the possession of fixed assets by the vertically integrated group as a whole is completely diversified.

Accordingly, it is apparently individual companies participating in the network that can most flexibly respond to the fluctuations in supply and demand in the market for the relevant product. However, evil practices such as "coercive sales" of goods from the upstream company to the downstream company, in which the transferred goods may be left as excess inventory and is said to be one of the defects of the single accounting settlement compared with the consolidated accounting settlement, may remain, so the efficiency of the relevant industry as a whole may be prevented from improving.

6.5 *Market transactions*

Finally, in the case where some companies in a network purchase goods or services in market transactions (i.e., in the automobile industry an iron & steel maker trades with overseas coal-mining company in the coal market),[6] such market transactions are outside the governance or control of the core company (integrator) because the suppliers may be likened to islands in the ocean called the market. There are no problems with the fact that some companies in the network are linked to the outside market via market transactions.

This is the boundary of the network organization. Similarly, the most downstream of the member companies of the network trade is with the consumer market of the end products. This also is the boundary of the network organization (Fig. 3).

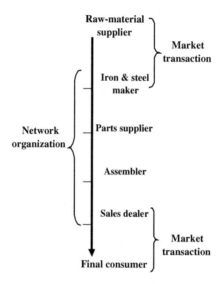

Fig. 3   Boundaries of network organization.

7   Design of an Incentive System for the Companies Participating in a Network

In a network organization, a participating company should not try to make a bargain with another company only to its advantage. Such a one-sided bargain will not last long. In transactions between companies, the so-called win-win relationship is necessary. This is the management control role of the core company and it is achieved by means of the profit-sharing system as incentive referred to in Section 6.1 Merger.

Profit sharing is attained by means of the internal transfer price, international transfer price, asset transfer price, parts price, or acquisition price, and so forth, to all of which I refer as *incentive price*. Upon seeing the shared profit offered by the core company based on this incentive system, prospective member companies decide on their own whether or not they will participate in the network. The prospective companies cannot be coerced into any decision. The only thing the integrator can do is to persuade them to participate using the incentive of shared profit.

However, with only the economic incentive of shared profit, it may be difficult to form a network organization that is desirable to the integrator. That is, prospective member companies of the network organization might not participate in the network organization if the incentive is merely a share of the profit. There is a problem that the profit obtained by maintaining independence and not participating in a complete coalition may be greater than the above-said shared profit. That is, a profit-sharing scheme that is satisfactory for all is difficult to design. Sometimes a partial coalition may be more profitable than a complete coalition.

However, in the case where a company that is the target for acquisition is a subsidiary in a consolidated business group, the possibility that the invitation to become a wholly owned subsidiary or be merged will be approved is higher. The approach taken in 2002 by Kunio Nakamura, president of Matsushita Electric (currently called Panasonic), was to acquire the full ownership of its five subsidiaries. The advantage of acquiring the full ownership of a company is that the president of the parent company can attend the stockholders' general meeting of the wholly owned subsidiary as a stockholder with 100% voting interest and it can fully accomplish the purpose of the parent company in the eventual restructuring of the group's organization (rationalization of the business of the group by splitting some of the businesses of its wholly owned subsidiaries, and so forth) using the centralized power of the integrator of the network organization.

Since an affiliated company of the consolidated business group cannot form a "partial coalition" of sub-group of affiliated companies departing from the control of the parent company, the profit sharing through the transaction price will be stable and easily accepted.

Now, the design of the profit-sharing system is essential to the construction of a network organization, but it is also an issue of management accounting.

The mechanism of profit sharing among the companies participating in a network is the theme of managerial accounting and the setting of the internal transfer prices of goods and services among the vertically allied companies and the setting of the profit-sharing system in the lump-sum total are also the problems to be solved.

The issue of setting the internal transfer prices refers to the way the business consignment prices are to be set at the joint of a value chain. The service consigner (or service recipient) would like to consign it at as low a price as possible, whereas the service consignee (or service provider) would like to provide it at as high a price as possible. Now, a profit-sharing scheme satisfactory to both parties is secured by sharing the profit according to the *degree of contribution* of each member company to the joint profit of the network.

Regarding the internal transfer price of the service, agreements such as "It shall be x% of the improvement in productivity resulting from the consignment of service" also imply sharing according to the degree of contribution (a proposal by Mr. Ohsai (2004) concerning the provision of personnel affairs services by IBM). For example, the difference in "the number of personnel engaged in an operation before receiving the service provided by another company (IBM)" and "the number of personnel sent to the relevant service section of the other company (IBM)" represents the magnitude of the improvement in productivity. Since this reflects the synergy effect, splitting the synergy effect fifty-fifty would be a method of profit sharing. The profit-sharing method is based on the same way of thinking as that which underlies the gain-allocation method in a cooperative game.

Furthermore, for the allotment of the risk of possessing the above fixed facility assets (which means bearing the fixed cost), the method of setting the prices of parts upon considering the allotment of risk involved in bearing the fixed cost among the assemblers (automakers) and parts suppliers (parts manufacturers) in the auto industry of Japan is also workable. This is the method to flexibly change the part price in response to the demand fluctuation of the part in question. In other words when the demand exceeded the estimated number of sales, the part price will be reduced, but when the demand became smaller than the estimated amount, the part price will be increased (for details see Monden & Nagao (1989) and Monden (1992)).

The issue of how to put the acquisition premium in the acquisition price in a corporate acquisition is also a synergy-sharing issue.

8 Determination of the Resource Allocation as *Task Control*: A Case of the Toyota Motor Group

In a network organization, the integrator can single handedly decide the daily resource allocation to and control a wide range of operational activities of the companies participating in the network.

The Toyota Motor Corporation, for example, carries out R&D, automobile assembly, and the production of some automobile parts on its own. However, the production of most parts is consigned to suppliers under its control and automobile sales are consigned to independent automobile dealers. (However, when each stage is observed in detail, for example, the development stage, there are some joint development projects undertaken together with suppliers under its control or other automakers. Also, there are cases where the final assembly is consigned to other companies in the group.) Although the relationships among the three parties are under Toyota's control, the market mechanism principle also works on the turn of model life.

Also, there is an information system connecting the three parties and they respond to the fluctuations in demand in accordance with the three-step order entry system of the sales companies (monthly order, 10-day order, and daily order) and realize JIT (just-in-time) production (that is, a system of producing salable products at salable times in salable amounts, aiming at a real-time supply-and-demand equilibrium). This is the ultimate system for speculative production. On the other hand, the built-to-order system adopted by Dell, in which assembly is begun upon receiving an order online, can attain a production that is perfectly balanced between supply and demand. Furthermore, the production itself is consigned to EMS companies in Taiwan, and so forth.

Notes

[1] The readers may think that the organization of inter-firm alliance or the network organization is the same as the so-called "intermediate organization." The concept and terminology of the

intermediate organization was first proposed by Imai, Itami, and Koike (1982).

They said that the intermediate organization would be located in the intermediate domain between the market and the internal organization (ibid. p. 126) based on the "theory of choice between a market and an organization" advocated by Ronald Harry Coase (Imai *et al.*, 1982, pp. 47–62). The nature of it is said as "mutual permeation of market principle and organization principle." In other words, applying the two measures of decision principle and membership of participants to both the *pure* market and the *pure* organization, the feature of the intermediate organization was described as a mixture of each respective nature of the above measures. Imai *et al.* (1982) said that by such mixture nature "the intermediate organization can utilize the merits of both pure market and pure internal organization by avoiding the defects of them" and it could be a basic organization theory of a business group.

The author admires that such original idea and the concept of intermediate organization was proposed about a quarter century ago.

[2] Then, which would become the core company (integrator) of a network organization and which would become the member companies in charge of the specialized functions under the overall control of the integrator?

In my opinion, since each company participating in a network organization is a legally independent entity, any company can be a core company *in any independent business network*. For example, let us assume that there are three business networks in the publishing industry:

1. Let us suppose that A, an American company, publishes books and journals on science, technology, and business, and sells them to foreign book importers of various countries and domestic book wholesalers. Since the publisher publishes the journals of learned societies on science, technology, and business of various countries, the editors of the journals in those countries provide the publisher with the edited copies. Therefore, publisher A forms network

AN together with foreign importers, domestic wholesalers, and the learned societies of various countries based on long-term tie-up agreements and it acts as the core company (integrator) of network AN.

2. Next, let us turn to B, a book importer in Japan and a member of network AN led by A. Importer B imports books and magazines from a number of publishers in various countries, including Great Britain, Germany, and Singapore, as well as from A, the United States publisher. As with A, B has long-term tie-up agreements with those publishers. B is the integrator of network BN formed under long-term tie-up agreements.

3. Lastly, let us focus on C, an American learned society and a member of AN, the network led by A. Let us suppose that C advertises to its members all over the world for research papers to be printed in its journal (i.e., calls for papers), reviews them, selects the papers to be printed, edits them, sends them to A for printing, bookbinding, and distribution of the journal to all over the world. Also, C has tie-up agreements with publishers other than A on the publication of scholarly books in serial form. Furthermore, C holds its annual congress meetings at various locations of the United States under a long-term agreement with a company engaged in organizing conferences. C has long-term tie-up agreements with various companies, including A, and it has a network, CN, with these companies as its members. Of course, C is the integrator of network CN.

Each of the above three business networks, AN, BN, and CN, is independent, but they overlap each other, and companies A, B, and C are the integrators of networks AN, BN, and CN, respectively. Each network differs in business type from the others; the integrator of each network designs the network from an independent perspective and it invites prospective member companies to join its own network. Such invitations may cross one another among the three networks. Each integrator has a predominant power in the decision-making process regarding resource allocation in the business area of its own network.

Apart from the above viewpoint, the central headquarters of a network that is not a certain company within the network can exist, and it is a neutral organ that can be established under mutual agreement of all members. For example, EU was established by yielding the sovereign powers and authorities of each nation to a super national headquarters. That headquarters is not charged on a certain country. We may learn how each of the United Nations, IMF, WTO, IOC, and so forth, is internally managed.

3 Three divisions of management roles in this section: *strategic decision*, *management control*, and *task control* are based on the management framework of Robert Anthony (see Anthony and Govindarajan (2006)).

4 Let us suppose a case in which, even after the merger of two companies in a network, the former two companies are integrated in the new company as upstream and downstream divisions, respectively. Even in this case, the *internal transfer prices* between the divisions function as a price incentive. If the "right of declination" from buying or selling internally is granted to both divisions, the supply division can sell goods to the outside market instead of conducting internal transfers, and the receiving division can purchase goods from the outside market instead of purchasing them from the inside. And again, the purpose of the transfer prices is to induce both divisions to participate. (However, usually the right of declination from selling internally is not granted to the supply division.)

5 The reason for full integration, other than maximizing the synergy effect, is that full integration allows the integrator to keep its trade secrets best, including proprietary information. When the integrator expects unacceptable loss due to the disclosure of its trade secrets as a result of a capital alliance with a company participating in the network, then, in order to eliminate the risk, the integrator acquires the company, places it under its control as an affiliate or fully merges it with itself (Galbraith, 2002).

6 Regarding the iron ore and coal, the resource company and the user company usually make a long-term trade contract, but the base of their bargaining is the spot price in the market.

References

Anthony, R and V Govindarajan (2006). *Management Control Systems*, 12th Ed., McGraw Hill.

Chandler, AD Jr. (1977). *The Visible Hand: The Managerial Revolution in American Business*. The Belknap Press of Harvard University Press.

Coase, RH (1937). The nature of the firm. *Economica*, 4, 386–405.

Cyert, RM and JG March (1963). *A Behavioral Theory of the Firm*. Prentice Hall.

Galbraith, JR (2002). *Designing Organization: An Executive Guide to Strategy, Structure, and Process*. New and revised Ed., John Wiley & Sons.

Higuchi, K (2000). Speed up establishment of the new Japanese style management. *Nihon Keizai Shinbun*, May 11 issue (in Japanese).

Imai, K, T Itami and K Koike (1982). *Economics in an Internal Organization*. Toyo Keizai, Inc (in Japanese).

Monden, Y (1992). *Cost Management in the New Manufacturing Age: Innovations in the Japanese Automobile Industry*. Productivity Press.

Monden, Y and N Nagao (1987/88). Full cost-based transfer pricing in the Japanese auto industry: risk-sharing and risk-spreading behavior. *Journal of Business Administration*, 17(1 and 2), 117–136 (Reproduced in Monden (1992), pp. 131–149).

Ohsai, T (2004). Economic reorganization for each functional unit. *Nihon Keizai Shinbun*, June 17 issue (in Japanese).

6

The Impact of Market Inefficiency on TOB in Japan

Tatsushi Yamamoto
Professor, Graduate School of Economics
Nagoya University

1 Introduction

Merger and acquisition (M&A) is a useful method of effective use of resources among firms. Through M&A, a firm creates organizational slack that can be used either for an expansion strategy (e.g., going into a new industrial sector) or for a restructuring strategy (e.g., decreasing debts by cutting personnel). Thus, M&A enables a firm to carry out a strategy that would otherwise be impossible (Yamamoto, 2002, pp. 164–165).

M&A also provides an effective method of corporate governance. If a firm is not managed well, then a stock price of the firm is generally low and the firm is likely to be a target of M&A. The threat of M&A forces a manager to make efforts; however, if the management fails to do so, it is excluded from the firm.

Accordingly, M&A is an important economic activity in terms of the effective use of resources among firms and corporate governance. For economic development in Japan, it is necessary to create an environment in which M&A is carried out without interruption.

A take-over bid (TOB) is an effective method of M&A. In this paper, we will examine a TOB that can be conducted without interruption by considering the causes of any such interruptions in the Japanese stock market. We will examine these problems from the viewpoint of market inefficiency.

Some empirical literature has pointed out anomalies, which indicate that the Japanese stock market is inefficient, at least in a short term (for instance, Kato, 2003). However, the short-term inefficient market has a great impact on a TOB, which has only a limited trading period. Therefore, market inefficiency is an important factor when considering a TOB.

We will also examine what a firm should do to conduct a TOB smoothly in Japan. Some literature has pointed out the inefficiency of the stock market and noted that the business environment in Japan is not favorable for M&A (for instance, Inoue, Kato, and Yamazaki, 2007). However, these obstacles cannot be removed immediately. It is, therefore, important to consider methods for the effective use of resources and valid corporate governance by which a firm can conduct a TOB smoothly, given the obstacles to M&A.

The remainder of the paper is organized as follows. In Section 2, we will examine two factors that cause the inefficiency in the market. In Section 3, we will examine some effective methods to conduct a TOB smoothly. In Section 4, we will present a case in which a TOB failed because of the inefficiency of the Japanese stock market. In the last section, we will summarize the discussion and we will state the conclusions.

2   Inefficiency of the Stock Market

2.1   *Causes of inefficiency of the market*

An efficient market is defined as a market in which prices always "fully reflect" available information (Fama, 1970, p. 383). Is the Japanese stock market efficient? It is not efficient, at least in the short term, because some empirical literature has pointed out various anomalies in the market. Therefore, it is necessary to take into account the factors that cause market inefficiency in order to examine its impact on a TOB.

Behavioral finance has received attention as an area that studies a stock price in an inefficient stock market. One of the main topics in behavioral finance is the effect of the psychology of investors on a stock price. We will make use of this knowledge in behavioral finance to consider a TOB in Japan.

Cross-shareholding is another characteristic factor that makes the Japanese market inefficient. Many Japanese firms hold the stocks of each other in order to have as many favorable shareholders as possible. In a cross-shareholding, a firm does not regard a short-term capital gain as important and it holds stocks for a relatively long time. In addition, this makes the market inefficient. Accordingly, it is necessary to take cross-shareholding into account when examining the impact of market inefficiency on a TOB in Japan.

2.2 Market inefficiency and knowledge in behavioral finance

2.2.1 Efficient market and behavioral finance

Efficient market hypothesis (EMH) argues that a stock price reflects the fundamental value of a firm and it is the sum of discounted future cash flows (for instance, Penman, 2004, pp. 74–84; Obinata, 2007, p. 198). This means that if a stock price diverges from its fundamental value, it will be readjusted immediately by arbitrage trading. In short, a stock price is determined only by the fundamental value of the firm and it is not influenced by the demand for its stocks.

Is the EMH true? There exist anomalies in the Japanese market, and these show that the demand for a stock has an impact on its price. Therefore, if the demand for a stock is high (low), then the price will become higher (lower), at least temporarily. Both in EMH and in behavioral finance, it is argued that in the long run, a stock price is efficient as it reflects all the information available. The major difference between EMH and behavioral finance is in the speed of adjustment of a stock price. In EMH, arbitrage trading immediately adjusts an inefficient stock price to its fundamental level. In behavioral finance, the adjustment takes some time, and the inefficient stock price remains in force for a certain period.

The basis of behavioral finance is irrationality of investors and shortage of arbitrage trading. The former means that activity of investors is in fact influenced by their psychological factors and, therefore, it is not always economically rational. The latter means that it takes a certain period to adjust an inefficient price because, given the psychological factors of investors and some institutional factors (e.g., short sale restrictions), sufficient arbitrage trading will not take place immediately.

2.2.2 Knowledge in behavioral finance

In behavioral finance, several concepts explain how a stock price has diverged from its fundamental value and how it has remained unadjusted for a certain period. Among them, we will focus on the following concepts.

Representativeness

A person is inclined to regard a realized phenomenon as a representative of the population because he or she has limited ability to process information. This is called representativeness. For instance, when a stock price becomes high, an investor believes that it represents the fundamental value of the firm.

Herding behavior

When many people take the same action, it is difficult for any one to take an action contrary to that action, even though it seems irrational. As a result, almost all the people will take the same action. This phenomenon is called herding behavior. It is often seen in a stock market and it causes a bubble and a sharp decline in a stock price.

Momentum

Generally, if a stock return has been high (low) in the past, its price is relatively high (low). In an efficient market, the stock price will experience a reversal and it will be adjusted to the fundamental level. However, if the price of a stock is relatively high (low), it will realize a high (low) return in the future. Together, these phenomena are called momentum.

Conservatism and overconfidence

A person is inclined not to update his or her belief about a population, even though an adverse phenomenon may occur. In addition if an action based on that belief has been successful in the past, a person will be less inclined to change that belief. This is called conservatism.

Roll's (1986) hubris hypothesis is a typical example. According to the hypothesis, a bidder sets a TOB price that is higher than the market price because the bidder has confidence in his or her ability to manage the target firm more effectively, based on some successful past experiences.

If investors influenced by the factors described above buy a specific stock, its price necessarily becomes much higher. Therefore, it is necessary to take behavioral factors into account when considering a TOB.

2.3 *Cross-shareholding among Japanese firms*

In Japan, there have existed several groups of firms called "Zaibatsu." In each of these groups, firms hold the stock of each other and this custom is known to foreign countries as "Keiretsu." In cross-holding groups, a firm does not regard a short-term capital gain as important and it holds the stocks for a relatively long time. This is one of the factors that make the stock market inefficient.

Cross-shareholding makes it difficult to conduct a successful TOB in several ways. First, cross-shareholding makes the liquidity of stocks low. Generally, a firm that is planning a TOB tries to buy stocks of the target firm before the TOB. However, low liquidity makes this difficult.

Second, cross-holding firms do not sell stocks, even if the price temporarily becomes higher. This means that arbitrage trading is not undertaken immediately to adjust the price. Thus, once the price has become relatively higher, it will remain high for a certain period. On the other hand, when the price becomes relatively lower, cross-holding firms buy stocks to hold. These actions make it difficult to conduct a successful TOB in Japan.

Third, cross-shareholding makes it difficult for an investor to make a short sale. When a stock price is relatively high, an investor generally borrows the stock and makes a short sale. However, the cross-holding firms are reluctant to lend the stocks. Therefore, there is not sufficient arbitrage trading to lower the price. This also makes it difficult to conduct a successful TOB in Japan.

The discussion above shows how cross-shareholding keeps a stock price relatively high. This is not because the stock price reflects an increase in the fundamental value of a firm, but because some mechanisms that adjust the stock price do not work in the market by cross-shareholding. For a TOB to succeed, it is generally necessary for a bidder to set a TOB price that is higher than the market price. Cross-shareholding in Japan makes such a success very difficult.

3 TOB Strategy

3.1 *Determination of TOB price and its effect*

TOB is a method of M&A that was established by the Financial Instruments and Exchange Law in Japan. In a TOB, a bidder (TOB firm) buys stocks of a target firm from shareholders at a price outside the stock market in a certain period. A TOB firm has to reveal the TOB period, the TOB price, and the number of stocks that it wishes to buy.

A TOB that is agreed to by the management of the target firm is called a "friendly TOB," otherwise, it is a "hostile TOB." It is an effective method of buying stocks, in both a friendly and a hostile TOB.

The most important problem for a TOB firm is determining a TOB price. Nobody knows the fundamental value of the target firm. Once the TOB price is revealed, investors are subject to the illusion that it represents the fundamental value of the target firm. On the bias of representativeness, the stock price will rise. A rational investor would consider the price to be relatively high. However, most investors do not sell out the shares. On the contrary, they engage in herding behavior and they buy the stocks. As a result, the price has positive momentum and it continues to rise.

Because investors obtain capital gains from the rise in the stock price, they become overconfident. Accordingly, even though some phenomena contrary to this belief may occur, they do not change it. Moreover, the conservatism of investors means that the stock price, which has diverged from its fundamental value, will be left unadjusted for a certain period.

As discussed above, when a TOB price is revealed, the stock price exhibits positive momentum toward it. Generally speaking, for a successful TOB, a firm must set the TOB price higher than the market price in the TOB period. If the firm sets a high price, the probability of success will be high, but this also creates a heavy financial burden on the TOB firm. On the other hand, if the firm sets a relatively low price, the probability of success will be lower.

Therefore, the determination of a TOB price is a very important issue. However, the success of TOB depends on the state of mind of investors, which is beyond the control of the TOB firm. Accordingly, determining the TOB price is a very difficult matter.

3.2   *Strategies for successful TOB*

To ensure a successful TOB, the best strategy of a firm is to obtain an agreement with the management of the target firm before the TOB and to realize a friendly TOB. In Japan, the custom of cross-shareholding is prevalent, and a large part of the stocks issued by the target firm is held by cross-holding firms. Accordingly, the success of a TOB depends considerably on whether they accept the TOB. The possibility of acceptance is higher in a friendly TOB.

One of the other benefits of a friendly TOB is that cross-holding firms do not always decide to sell or hold based on the TOB price alone. In other words, it is highly probable that in a friendly TOB, the cross-holding firms will accept the TOB even if the TOB price is not sufficiently high. In fact, there have been cases in which cross-holding firms sold the stocks, even though the TOB price was lower than the market price (one of the examples is the TOB of Nippon Broadcasting System, Inc. by Fuji Television Network Inc. in 2005). This is of great benefit for the TOB firm, because it mitigates the difficulties of determining the TOB price considerably.

Another benefit of a friendly TOB is that it enables the TOB firm to save considerable costs (e.g., the costs of litigation), which tend to occur in the case of a hostile TOB, because the target firm has not taken any defenses (e.g., poison pill, crown jewel, and so forth), and a white knight does not appear.

However, the management of a target firm does not always agree to a TOB. In this case, the TOB then becomes hostile, and the TOB firm cannot obtain the benefits of a friendly TOB, as described above. The second-best strategy is to give some rents to the management of the target firm, and thus, obtain their agreement on the TOB. The rents can be either monetary (e.g., golden parachute) or nonmonetary (e.g., a position in the management).

If the TOB price is relatively high, there is no reason why shareholders of the target firm should reject the TOB. Accordingly, when the price is relatively high and the management of the target firm rejects it, they are giving higher priority to the private benefits, which they will obtain from the failure of the TOB, than to the profit of shareholders. In this case, if the TOB firm promises to give the management at least as large benefit as they would receive from the failure of the TOB, then they will agree on the TOB.

What should a TOB firm do if the management rejects even this offer? It is not true that all the management act only for their private benefits. However, it should be noted that they do not act for the profit of shareholders. Some Japanese managements act on the belief that they must retain their independence.

It is no use giving rents to the management. In such a case, the TOB firm cannot avoid a hostile TOB. When a friendly TOB is abandoned, the only thing that will encourage the cross-holding firms to sell the stocks is the TOB price. Such a TOB price must be sufficiently high to induce them to abandon their long-term relationship with the target firm and accept the TOB. Even the cross-holding firms cannot ignore the TOB price, if it is sufficiently high, because if they do so, the management of the cross-holding firms are exposed to serious danger of being sued by their shareholders (e.g., shareholder litigation).

However, it is risky for the TOB firm to offer a very high TOB price. First, it increases the financial burden on the TOB firm. Second, it raises the stock price of the target firm. Third, if the TOB firm sets a very high TOB price, then investors may be wary of the hubris of the management of the TOB firm and the stock price of the TOB firm will probably decrease.

4 A TOB Case in Japan

In this section, we will examine a case in which a TOB failed due to the psychological factors of investors and the custom of cross-shareholding in Japan. The contents of this section are based on the articles in the Nikkei from July 2 to September 8, 2006.

Recently, the profitability of the Japanese paper industry has declined, following a decrease in demand. Most firms in the industry had over capacity and they had to restructure, including Oji Paper Co., Ltd (Oji), the biggest paper manufacturing firm in Japan.

Oji offered some business integration to Hokuetsu Paper Mills, Ltd (Hokuetsu) in March 2006, and on July 3, it informed Hokuetsu that it was prepared to purchase 10% of the outstanding stocks of Hokuetsu. Oji wanted to obtain the Niigata factory of Hokuetsu, which had a highly productive machine. After the integration, Oji intended to restructure the business by making the best use of the factory. First, Oji attempted a friendly M&A. However, Hokuetsu rejected the offer and on July 21, it announced an allocation of new shares to Mitsubishi Corporation (Mitsubishi Co.). The flotation price was 607 yen a share, and Mitsubishi Co. would obtain 24.44% of the voting stocks of Hokuetsu. It was announced that the purpose of the allocation was to raise funds to invest in the Niigata factory (from the formal home page of Mitsubishi Co; http://www. mitsubishicorp.com/jp/pdf/pr/mcpr060721p.pdf), but in reality, it was to prevent Hokuetsu from being taken over.

The flotation price of 607 yen was much lower than the lowest market price on July 21, which was 632 yen, and it was not changed despite an announcement by Oji that the TOB price would be 860 yen. Obviously, the allocation damaged the profits of the existing shareholders in Hokuetsu. In short, the management of Hokuetsu prevented the firm from being taken over by taking advantage of the cross-shareholding, even though by doing so, it damaged the profits of the existing shareholders.

Finally, Oji gave up on a friendly TOB, and on August 2, it started a TOB for Hokuetsu as a last resort. This was the beginning of its hostile TOB. It attracted the attention of people as a hostile TOB by the biggest firm in the Japanese paper industry. The TOB period was from August 2 to September 4 and the TOB price was 800 yen a share. The aim of Oji was to obtain a little more than 50% of the voting stocks. Oji reduced the TOB price from 860 yen to 800 yen because it considered that the flotation price of 607 yen for the allocation of new shares was too low. It is evident that this allocation would also damage the profits of the existing shareholders in Hokuetsu.

Unexpectedly, Nippon Paper Industries Co., Ltd (Nippon Paper), the second biggest firm in the industry, announced that it had obtained 8.85% of the voting stocks of Hokuetsu between July 28 and August 8. This was the appearance of a white knight. Nippon Paper obviously aimed to prevent the monopoly of Oji in the industry.

The stock price of Hokuetsu had increased since July 23, when Oji announced that it was going to make a TOB for Hokuetsu. The price was 635 yen on Friday, July 21 (the last trading day before the announcement of the TOB). The announcement came on Sunday, July 23. The stock price was 735 yen on July 24, 789 yen on July 25, and 802 yen on July 28, i.e., higher than the TOB price. The substantial rise in the stock price can be attributed to the recognition by investors that the TOB price was representative of the fundamental value of Hokuetsu and the herding behavior by the investors had created a positive momentum. Finally, on August 8, the price reached 855 yen, the highest in the TOB period, when Nippon Paper announced that it had obtained 8.85% of the voting stocks of Hokuetsu.

In the end, only 5.33% of the shareholders in Hokuetsu accepted the TOB and Oji failed in its TOB. The Nikkei, August 24, 2006 showed how the institutional shareholders in Hokuetsu reacted to the TOB before August 24. It is certain that profits of the cross-holding firms were damaged by the allocation of new stocks to Mitsubishi Co. However, most of them were in favor of the management of Hokuetsu and they refused the TOB. It seems that they refused it because they were essentially against the hostile TOB and not because they were unsatisfied with the TOB price.

This is one case in which the psychology of investors and the custom of cross-shareholding in Japan resulted in the failure of a hostile TOB. The aim of the TOB was to decrease over capacity and to raise profitability by integration. Moreover, the TOB price was sufficiently high, but even then it failed. This fact shows the following. First, a friendly TOB is almost a necessary condition for the success of TOB in Japan. Second, the custom of cross-shareholding creates a serious impediment to a hostile TOB. Finally, the psychology of investors has large effects on the stock price and this makes it difficult for a TOB firm to determine the TOB price.

5 Concluding Remarks

M&A is a useful method of effective use of resources among firms and corporate governance. For economic development in Japan, it is necessary to create an environment in which M&A is carried out without interruption. In light of this view, we examined a TOB that can be carried out without interruption in the Japanese stock market by considering the causes of such interruption. As a result, we found that a TOB in Japan was greatly interrupted by market inefficiency and this inefficiency was caused by the psychology of investors and the custom of cross-shareholding.

Next, we examined what a TOB firm should do to conduct a TOB smoothly, given the market inefficiency. We found that the best strategy is to obtain an agreement of the management of the target firm to the TOB; this means a friendly TOB. In case the TOB firm cannot obtain such an agreement, the second-best strategy is to give some rents to the management and to induce them to agree to the TOB. Rents can be either monetary or nonmonetary. If the management agrees to the TOB, the TOB firm can obtain benefits of a friendly TOB. In case rents fail, the last resort is a hostile TOB. This means giving up a friendly takeover and setting a TOB price that is sufficiently high. In this way, the TOB firm puts some pressure on the management of the cross-holding firms to sell the stocks by taking advantage of the threat that if they reject the TOB, they may be sued in shareholder litigation. However, a hostile TOB should be avoided as much as possible not only because it makes it impossible for the TOB firm to obtain the benefits of a friendly TOB but also because it is very costly.

References

Fama, EF (1970). Efficient capital markets: a review of theory and empirical work. *Journal of Finance*, 25(2), 383–423.

Inoue, K, H Kato and T Yamazaki (2007). Insurance company puzzle in Japan. *Securities Analysts Journal*, 45(12), 114–123 (in Japanese).

Kato, H (2003). *Behavioral Finance*. Asakura Publishing Co., Tokyo (in Japanese).

Obinata, T (2007). *Advanced Financial Accounting*, Chuokeizai-Sha Inc., Tokyo (in Japanese).

Penman, SH (2004). *Financial Statement Analysis and Security Valuation*, 2nd Ed. McGraw Hill, New York.

Roll, R (1986). The hubris of corporate takeovers. *Journal of Business*, 59(2), 197–216.

Yamamoto, T (2002). *Theory on the Effects of Strategies and Accounting Information*. Chuokeizai-Sha Inc., Tokyo (in Japanese).

7

A Survey of Public-to-Private Buy-out Transactions in Japan

Keiichi Sugiura

Representative Director, Japan Buy-out Research Institute

1 Introduction

In recent years, public-to-private buy-out deals have increased rapidly in Japan. In particular, since 2005, it is notable that many large-scale transactions were executed. Such mega transactions include Pokka Corporation, World, Skylark, Q'SAI, Toshiba Ceramics, and Rex Holdings.

The purpose of this paper is to clear the feature of public-to-private buy-out transactions in Japan. This paper is organized as follows. The first section explains the trend of public-to-private buy-outs in Japan. The second section classifies the public-to-private buy-out transactions in Japan. The third section analyzes the financial package of the 46 cases of public-to-private buy-outs in Japan. Finally, some conclusions are drawn.

2 Trends of Public-to-Private Buy-outs in Japan

Figure 1 shows the trends of public-to-private buy-out deals in Japan. In principal, the transaction value includes the amount of buying price (purchase price per ordinary share × total shares purchased) and it does not include the various expenses such as legal fee. But in this statistics, the value of Bellsystem24's transaction include the amount of third party allotment of shares which is executed in pre-TOB stage and stock acquisition from CSK Corporation. According

Year	Number	Value (Billion yen)
2000	1	8
2001	4	28
2002	1	6
2003	6	74
2004	1	230
2005	5	260
2006	6	461
2007	17	446
2008 (half year)	5	274
Total	46	1,787

Fig. 1   Trends of public-to-private buy-out deals in Japan.

to Japan Buy-out Research Institute (2008), 17 deals were executed and the past total value reached 1.5 trillion yen in 2007. From January 2008 to June 2008, 5 deals including the deal of Tokyo Star Bank are executed.

3   Classification of Public-to-Private Transactions in Japan

Public-to-Private transactions in Japan is divided into five types: 1. divestment type; 2. business succession type; 3. secondary buyouts; 4. strategic going-private type; and 5. protection against hostile takeover type.

3.1   *Divestment type*

The divestment type transaction occurs based on the factor of the selling needs by a parent company. There are circumstances of parent company that look like the need to restructure its assets in order to reduce interest-bearing debt or to spin out a non-core business. In addition to such circumstances, divestment type public-to-private transactions are executed when buy-out firms and management teams wish to take the target company private.

Figure 2 shows the case of divestment type public-to-private buy-out transactions in Japan. The typical case is Kiriu Corporation,

Year	Deal name	Business	Vendor (proportion of shares)
3/2001	Tocalo	Manufacturing	Nittetsu Shoji (60.43%)
12/2001	Kiriu Corporation	Manufacturing	Nissan Motor Co. (36.7%)
3/2003	Kokura Enterprise	Real estate	Sumitomo Metal Industries (58.30%)
12/2003	Toshiba Tungaloy (now Tungaloy)	Manufacturing	Toshiba (36.98%)
8/2005	Gakken Credit	Services	Gakken (65.91%)
10/2005	Kinrei Corporation	Services	Osaka Gas (44.33%) OG Capital (30.48%)
12/2006	Toshiba Ceramics (now Covalent Materials Corporation)	Manufacturing	Toshiba (40.40%)
11/2007	Simplex Investment Advisors	Real estate	Nikko Cordial Holdings (29.41%) Nikko Cordial Group (13.03%)

Fig. 2   Divestment type deals.

an auto parts manufacturer. Nissan Motor Co., a car manufacturer, sold Kiriu Corporation to Unison Capital. In the first half of the 2000s, Nissan Motor had sold many subsidiaries on the policy "Nissan Revival Plan." Another case includes Toshiba Tungaloy (now Tungaloy). In 2003, Toshiba sold Toshiba Tungaloy to Nomura Principal Finance as part of policy of concentrating on core business.

3.2   *Business succession type*

The business succession type occurs based on the factor of the needs by family owner. In such a situation, founder-manager realizes founder's profit after selling the business to financial buyer. The common feature with divestment type is in the needs of the seller.

Figure 3 shows the case of business succession type public-to-private buy-out transactions in Japan. The typical case is Daimon (now MineMart), a retail chain of discount stores specializing in alcoholic drinks. In the case of Daimon, founder of advanced age sold the company to Unison Capital in 2000. In 2006, founder family of KYU-SAI, a manufacturer of health foods centered on Q'SAI Chlorophyll Juice, sold the company to the investment consortium composed of

Year	Deal name	Business	Vendor (proportion of shares)
9/2000	MineMart	Retailing	Founding family (31.93%) Asset management company (22.87%)
9/2001	ORIX Facilities	Services	Asset management company (21.72%) Founding family (20.55%)
3/2002	UHT	Manufacturing	Founding family (33.69%)
12/2006	KYUSAI	Manufacturing	Major shareholders including founding family (64.06%)
11/2007	Thanks Japan Corporation	Retailing	Founding family (19.1%)

Fig. 3   Business succession type deals.

Year	Deal name	Business	Vendor (Proportion of shares)
3/2008	Tokyo Star Bank	Bank	Lone Star Funds (68.1%)

Fig. 4   Secondary buy-out deals.

NIF SMBC Ventures, Japan Industrial Partners and Polaris Principal Finance.

3.3   *Secondary buy-outs*

Secondary buy-outs occur based on the factor of the sale needs by buy-out funds (Fig. 4). Tokyo Star Bank was listed to the Tokyo Stock Exchange in 2005. But the Tokyo Star Bank executed the going-private transaction in 2008 with the sale needs by Lone Star Funds, which is a majority shareholder. In recent years, the method of PIPEs (private investment in public equities) that the buy-out funds invest for the listed company becomes popular and there is opportunity of going-private transactions.

3.4   *Strategic going-private type*

Strategic type public-to-private deals is executed not as a result of sale demand of the major shareholders but because the incumbent management team wishes to obtain managerial flexibility. As many

Year	Deal name	Business
8/2001	CCI	Manufacturing
3/2003	Roki Techno	Manufacturing
9/2003	Kito	Manufacturing
9/2003	Shinwa	Manufacturing
10/2003	Foodx Globe	Services
11/2004	Bellsystem24	Services
9/2005	WORLD	Wholesaling
9/2005	POKKA Corporation	Manufacturing
12/2005	Technol Eight	Manufacturing
7/2006	Skylark	Services
8/2006	Yagi Corporation	Wholesaling
12/2006	Shinmei Electric	Manufacturing
12/2006	REX Holdings	Services and retailing
2/2007	Ryowa Life Create	Real estate
2/2007	ASAHIDANKE	Manufacturing
2/2007	NIPPON FILING	Manufacturing
3/2007	Tsubaki Nakashima	Manufacturing
3/2007	Sunstar	Manufacturing
4/2007	Meikoshokai	Manufacturing
6/2007	PREC Institute	Services
7/2007	BELX	Services
10/2007	Sanko	Real estate
10/2007	Nippon Logistech Corporation	Logistics
12/2007	UNION PAINT	Manufacturing
12/2007	HORIUCHI COLOR	Services
12/2007	CYBIRD Holdings	Services
12/2007	PATLITE Corporation	Manufacturing
1/2008	HANSHIN Dispensing Pharmacy	Retailing
1/2008	KRAFT	Retailing
5/2008	Ida technos	Construction
6/2008	NIPPON DOKENCO	Construction

Fig. 5   Strategic going-private type deals.

public companies in Japan worry about the disadvantage of maintaining staying public, the public-to-private deals concluded have been of this type. Figure 5 shows the strategic type going-private transactions.

3.5   *Protection against hostile takeover type*

Protection against hostile takeover-type deals arise when the management of a public company that is subject to a hostile bid from a green mailer or similar ask an investment company such as a buy-out

Year	Deal name	Business
2/3/2007	SunTelephone	Services

Fig. 6   Protection against Hostile takeovers type deals.

fund to act as a white knight in a friendly buy-out plan (Fig. 6). In 2007, the SunTelephone was executed going-private transaction after the activist fund prepared a hostile takeover.

4   Public-to-Private Deals and Financial Package

Most of the deals that were executed in the early market were financial sponsor-backed transactions. And the members of equity sponsor were pioneer players such as Unison Capital and Nomura Principal Finance. The member of debt provider was some Japanese mega bank. In recent years, the new entry buy-out funds are executing the public-to-private buy-out transactions and the member of equity provider becomes various (Fig. 7). In addition, as many foreign investment banks enter the debt arranger market, the member of debt provider becomes various. In the type of finance, some mezzanine players provide a mezzanine finance such as the preference shares, subordinated bond, subordinated loan, and buy-out finance method, which is diversified. The most attracting attention matters are the increase of no financial sponsor-backed transactions.

5   Conclusion

This paper views the characteristics of public-to-private buy-out deals in Japan. It reveals that such deals fall into five categories: (1) divestment type, (2) business succession type, (3) secondary buy-outs, (4) strategic type, and (5) protection-against-hostile takeover type. Among the five categories, strategic type deals are the most common. It also clears that the members of equity provider and debt provider are diversified. Subjects of future study include measuring the impact and performance of going-private transactions.

Date	Deal name	TOB value billion yen	Equity provider (financial sponsor)	Debt provider (including bridge loan)
25/9/2000	MineMart	8.2	Unison Capital	Nihon Kogyo Bank (loan commitment of 11.7 billion yen)
12/3/2001	Tocal	6.3	JAFCO	Tokai Bank (loan commitment of 6.9 billion yen)
30/8/2001	CCI	9.9	Nomura Principal Finance	Nomura Principal Finance (loan commitment of 10.4 billion yen)
21/9/2001	ORIX Facilities	4.3	ORIX	ORIX (loan commitment of 6.5 billion yen)
27/12/2001	KIRIU Corporation	7.0	Unison Capital	Aozora Bank (loan commitment of 8.5 billion yen)
29/3/2002	UHT	5.7	Nomura Principal Finance	Nomura Principal Finance (loan commitment of 6.3 billion yen)
19/3/2003	Roki Techno	6.8	Raffia Capital	Shinsei Bank (loan commitment of 5.8 billion yen)
27/3/2003	Kokura Enterprise	6.6	Advantage Partners	Mizuho Bank (loan commitment of 5.35 billion yen)
3/9/2003	Kito	5.2	The Carlyle Group	Sumitomo Mitsui Banking Corporation (loan commitment of 7 billion yen)
25/9/2003	Shinwa	8.0	Raffia Capital	Shinsei Bank (loan commitment of 5.8 billion yen)
24/10/2003	Foodx Globe	11.7	AC Capital	Mizuho Bank
18/12/2003	Toshiba Tungaloy	35.7	Nomura Principal Finance	Nomura Principal Finance (loan commitment of 39 billion yen)

Fig. 7   Summary of TOBs in public-to-private buy-out deals in Japan.

Date	Deal name	TOB value billion yen	Equity provider (financial sponsor)	Debt provider (including bridge loan)
2/11/2004	Bellsystem24	230	Nikko Principal Investments Japan	Nikko Principal Investments Japan (loan commitment of 88 billion yen)
16/8/2005	Gakken Credit	7.9	NIF SMBC Ventures	NIF Corporate Management (loan commitment of 10 billion yen)
26/9/2005	WORLD	208	No financial sponsor transaction (pure management buy-out) [Preference share] Chuo Mitsui Capital	[Senior loan] Sumitomo Mitsui Banking Corporation (loan commitment of 88.25 billion yen) Sumitomo Trust & Banking (loan commitment of 44.125 billion yen) Aozora Bank (loan commitment of 44.125 billion yen) [Subordinated bonds] Chuo Mitsui Capital
27/9/2005	POKKA Corporation	23.4	Advantage Partners CITIC Capital Partners	[Senior loan] Sumitomo Mitsui Banking Corporation (loan commitment of 17 billion yen) [Subordinated loan] Tokio Marine & Nichido Fire Insurance (loan commitment of 5 billion yen)
28/10/2005	Kinrei Corporation	14.6	Cas Capital	Sumitomo Mitsui Banking Corporation (loan commitment of 11.35 billion yen)
15/12/2005	Technol Eight	6.0	No financial sponsor transaction (pure management buy-out)	Chuo Mitsui Trust and Banking Company (loan commitment of 7 billion yen)

Fig. 7 (*Continued*)

Date	Deal name	TOB value billion yen	Equity provider (financial sponsor)	Debt provider (including bridge loan)
21/7/2006	Skylark	257	Nomura Principal Finance CVC Asia Pacific (Japan)	Mizuho Bank (loan commitment of 220 billion yen)
29/8/2006	Yagi Corporation	5.0	No financial sponsor transaction (pure management buy-out)	Nomura Capital Investment (loan commitment of 6 billion yen)
1/12/2006	KYUSAI	61.4	[Ordinary share] NIF SMBC Ventures Polaris Principal Finance Japan Industrial Partners [Preference share] Shiomizaka Capital	[Senior loan] Sumitomo Mitsui Banking Corporation (loan commitment of 33 billion yen) [Subordinated loan] Shinsei Bank (loan commitment of 3 billion yen) DBJ Corporate Mezzanine Partners (loan commitment of 4 billion yen) Shiomizaka Capital (loan commitment of 4 billion yen)
7/12/2006	Shinmei Electric	8.8	NIF SMBC Ventures	Sumitomo Mitsui Banking Corporation (loan commitment of 9.9 billion yen)
11/12/2006	Toshiba Ceramics	83.1	[Ordinary share] Unison Capital The Carlyle Group [Preference share] Chuo Mitsui Capital	Sumitomo Mitsui Banking Corporation (loan commitment of 26 billion yen) Mizuho Corporate Bank (loan commitment of 26 billion yen) The Royal Bank of Scotland plc (loan commitment of 13 billion yen)

Fig. 7 (*Continued*)

Date	Deal name	TOB value billion yen	Equity provider (financial sponsor)	Debt provider (including bridge loan)
19/12/2006	REX Holdings	45.7	Advantage Partners	[Senior loan] Sumitomo Mitsui Banking Corporation (loan commitment of 22.5 billion yen) [Mezzanine finance] Credit Suisse Group (loan commitment of 38 billion yen)
7/2/2007	Ryowa Life Create	43.4	Revamp Corporation Lehman Brothers Group Toranomon Capital	Lehman Brothers Group (loan commitment of 44 billion yen)
8/2/2007	ASAHIDANKE	2.2	No financial sponsor transaction (pure management buy-out)	The Hokkaido Bank (loan commitment of 1.2 billion yen) North Pacific Bank (loan commitment of 0.7 billion yen) Asahikawa Shinkin Bank (loan commitment of 0.25 billion yen) The Sapporo Bank (loan commitment of 0.25 billion yen)
14/2/2007	NIPPON FILING	4.6	No financial sponsor transaction (pure management buy-out)	Sumitomo Mitsui Banking Corporation (loan commitment of 5.1 billion yen)

Fig. 7   (*Continued*)

Date	Deal name	TOB value billion yen	Equity provider (financial sponsor)	Debt provider (including bridge loan)
2/3/2007	SunTelephone	33.9	Japan Industrial Partners Bain Capital Partners, LLC	Mizuho Corporate Bank (loan commitment of 30 billion yen)
2/3/2007	Tsubaki Nakashima	101.4	Nomura Principal Finance	Nomura Capital Investment (loan commitment of 75 billion yen)
23/3/2007	Sunstar	18.5	No financial sponsor transaction (pure management buy-out)	Nomura Capital Investment (loan commitment of 40 billion yen)
26/4/2007	Meikoshokai	20.6	JAFCO	Sumitomo Trust & Banking (loan commitment of 19.5 billion yen)
22/6/2007	PREC Institute	0.8	No financial sponsor transaction (pure management buy-out)	Bank of Tokyo-Mitsubishi UFJ (loan commitment of 2 billion yen)
3/7/2007	BELX	6.0	No financial sponsor transaction (pure management buy-out)	Sumitomo Mitsui Banking Corporation (loan commitment of 6.373 billion yen)
16/10/2007	Sanko	3.5	DBJ Business Investment	Sumitomo Mitsui Banking Corporation (loan commitment of 1.87 billion yen) Development Bank of Japan (loan commitment of 1.31 billion yen)

Fig. 7   (*Continued*)

Date	Deal name	TOB value billion yen	Equity provider (financial sponsor)	Debt provider (including bridge loan)
22/10/2007	Nippon Logistech Corporation	1.7	No financial sponsor transaction (pure management buy-out)	Resona Bank (loan commitment of 3.75 billion yen)
16/11/2007	Simplex Investment Advisors	154.2	The Goldman Sachs Group Aetos Capital, LLC	Isehara, LLC (loan commitment of 158.4 billion yen)
26/11/2007	Thanks Japan Corporation	8.3	No financial sponsor transaction (pure management buy-out) [Preference share] Sakigake Investments	Sumitomo Mitsui Banking Corporation (loan commitment of 4.5 billion yen)
20/12/2007	CYBIRD Holdings	15.6	The Longreach Group	Aozora Bank (loan commitment of 6 billion yen)
21/12/2007	UNION PAINT	1.2	No financial sponsor transaction (pure management buy-out)	Bank of Tokyo-Mitsubishi UFJ (loan commitment of 1.4 billion yen)
25/12/2007	HORIUCHI COLOR	5.4	No financial sponsor transaction (pure management buy-out)	Nomura Capital Investment (loan commitment of 6.6 billion yen)

Fig. 7 (*Continued*)

Date	Deal name	TOB value billion yen	Equity provider (financial sponsor)	Debt provider (including bridge loan)
26/12/2007	PATLITE Corporation	21.5	Palace Capital	Chuo Mitsui Trust and Banking Company (loan commitment of 20 billion yen)
8/1/2008	HANSHIN Dispensing Pharmacy	3.3	Valiant Partners	Bank of Tokyo-Mitsubishi UFJ (loan commitment of 4.47 billion yen) Aozora Bank (loan commitment of 2.23 billion yen)
1/2/2008	KRAFT	17.3	No financial sponsor transaction (pure management buy-out)	Sumitomo Mitsui Banking Corporation (loan commitment of 22.3 billion yen)
14/3/2008	Tokyo Star Bank	247.7	Advantage Partners	Merrill Lynch Japan Securities Bayerische Hypo-und Vereinsbank AG Calyon, Tokyo Branch Credit Suisse Group Shinsei Bank (loan commitment of 169.9 billion yen)
22/5/2008	Ida technos	1.5	No financial sponsor transaction (pure management buy-out)	Sumitomo Mitsui Banking Corporation (loan commitment of 2.91 billion yen)
24/6/2008	NIPPON DOKENCO	3.8	No financial sponsor transaction (pure management buy-out)	Sumitomo Mitsui Banking Corporation (loan commitment of 7.16 billion yen)

Fig. 7 (*Continued*)

References

Japan Buy-out Research Institute (2008). *Japan Buy-out Market Review 2008*, Japan Buy-out Research Institute.

Sugiura, K (2006). The characteristics of public to private buy-outs in Japan. *Journal of Creative Management*, 2(1), 171–184 (in Japanese).

Watanabe, H (2004). *Examination of Public to Private Management Buy-out/In Activity in Japan*, Dissertation, (M.B.A.) University of Nottingham.

8
Do M&As in Japan Increase Shareholder Value?

Kotaro Inoue

Associate Professor, Graduate School of Business Administration
Keio University

1　Introduction

This paper examines recent empirical studies that assess whether mergers and acquisitions (M&A) in Japan increase shareholder value and what the economic reasons underlie such effects. It also summarizes a series of analysis in papers I have published recently and it aims to report the essence rather than details of the analyses.

In the United States, the effect of M&As on shareholder value has been the most heavily studied. Therefore, I report the effect of M&As in Japan by comparing it with the effect of M&As in the United States, in order to project a clearer picture to the readers. I report the conditions and characteristics of the M&A market in Japan and its economic efficiency.

I show that the importance of M&As has suddenly increased from the second half of the 1990s in Japan and that deregulation of industries appears to be the major cause for such change. I also show that in addition to the shareholder value of target firms, the shareholder value of the acquiring firms increases as a result of the less intense competition in the M&A market in Japan, compared with that of the United States, and that there is a business synergy in the background of increasing shareholder value. These results are based on the empirical results of M&As from 1990 to 2002. However, the distribution of the wealth effect from M&As among shareholders does not change even when we extend the analysis to the sample, which covers deals announced until the end of 2007. This suggests that although the number of M&A deals is increasing rapidly in the last ten years, the M&A market in Japan is still less competitive than that in the United States.

It is clear that in Japan, where industries have been protected by regulations and the main bank system, the M&A market does not assume importance until the mid-1990s. Over the past ten years, M&As have played an important role by serving as countermeasures against changes in the business environment. The characteristics of the M&A market in Japan are similar to those in the United States and they are not necessarily unique. The evidence presented show that in a market that undergoes deregulation, M&As serve as an important and effective competitive strategy for a firm.

2   The State of the M&A Market in Japan

Inoue and Kato (Inoue, 2002; Inoue and Kato, 2003, 2006) investigate M&As between public firms in Japan between 1990 and 2002 in detail. A transition of M&A between public firms in Japan is shown in Fig. 1.

Figure 1 shows that although the M&A market did not play an important role in Japan till the mid-1990s, it increased in importance rapidly in the late 1990s. The timing of this change is coincident with the timing of the full-scale deregulation of industries, including the "Japanese Big Bang," in financial industries. In fact, when we classify the firms that participated in M&A deals between 1990 and 2002, we notice that they usually represent the industries wherein large-scale deregulation has taken place (finance, healthcare, and oil), the industries wherein excess supply decreases the product or service prices (paper manufacture, cement, and marine business), and the industries wherein industrial reorganization is required because of the intense overseas competition (chemistry).

Coase (1937) pointed out that a firm adjusts the boundary of its own business operations such that its transaction costs can be minimized when it encounters a change in the market environment. In line with such a perspective, in the United States, Mitchell and

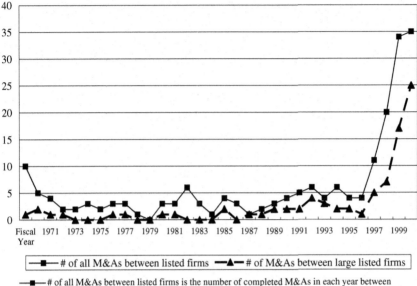

— ■ — # of all M&As between listed firms   — ▲ — # of M&As between large listed firms

— ■ — # of all M&As between listed firms is the number of completed M&As in each year between listed firms on stock exchanges in Japan (excluding listed firms on JASDAQ). — ▲ — # of M&As between large listed firms is the number of completed M&As between listed firms of which book value of equity exceed 5 billion Yen.

Fig. 1   Number of M&A deals between listed firms in Japan.

Mulherin (1996) and Andrade, Mitchell, and Stafford (2001) high-light the trend of M&As concentrating in a specific industry at a specific period due to industry-specific shocks such as deregulations, technological innovations, or increasing overseas competition. As mentioned earlier, the same tendency is observed in Japan. While the industries depended on protection from regulations before the 1980s, a Japanese firm can survive independently without M&A activities. After the mid-1990s, M&As constitute an indispensable measure for Japanese firms for survival after deregulation has been implemented.

Andrade *et al.* (2001) show that between 1970s and 1990s, the price-to-book ratio (PBR) of acquirer firms exceeded the PBR of target firms in two-thirds of its more than 4,000 samples. Inoue (2008) indicated that the PBR of acquirer firms exceeded the PBR of target firms in two-thirds of the M&As between public firms in Japan between 1990 and 2002. Thus, both in the United States and in Japan, M&As are used as a measure to counter industry-specific shocks in the deregulated competitive market; firms that are considered to be rather efficient by the stock market become acquirers and dismiss firms regarded as inefficient. This corroborates that M&As in Japan are transactions that meet economic efficiency.

Even after 2002, the M&A market in Japan continued to grow. The number of M&As between listed firms in the five years, 2003 to 2007, amounted to nearly 400. This number is about three times as many as the number of deals in the previous five years, 1998 to 2002. Further, acquisitions by investment funds are also increasing rapidly after the year 2000. Thus, it is for the last ten years that the M&A market in Japan has grown and the characteristics of the market has also changed; previously, there used to be mergers well coordinated by large stakeholders such as main banks and keiretsu, and now they are mainly acquisitions based on market principles.

3 Do M&As in Japan Increase Shareholder Value?

The impact of the announcement of an M&A on shareholder value is considered by economic researchers to be an objective and important indicator with which to assess value creation and the economic efficiency of M&A activities. Even when a deal is supported by an economic rationale, if the deal destroys the acquirer's shareholder value, it is not supported by the shareholders. Thus, it is important for the development of the M&A market that, on an average, M&As increase shareholder value.

Figure 2 shows the effect of M&As in Japan on shareholder value, which is compared with that in the United States. The effect on shareholder value is shown in cumulative abnormal return (CAR) of acquirer firms and target firms in the three days around the day of the initial announcement of the deals. The abnormal return is measured by the excess return to the bench mark portfolio in each market.

Although the shareholders' return for acquirer firms almost breaks even, it tends to be positive in Japan and negative in the United States. On the other hand, on an average, for target firms, it is significantly positive and also for the combination of acquirer and

	Japan		United States
	1990–2002	2003–2007	1973–1998
Combined	1.8%*	n.a.	1.8%*
Acquirer	1.5%	1.2%*	−0.7%
Target	4.4%*	8.2%*	16.0%*
No. Obs.	137	379	3,688

Result of Japan (1990–2002) is from Inoue (2002) and Inoue and Kato (2006). Result of Japan (2003–2007) is author's own analysis for this paper. Result of United States is from Andrade *et al.* (2001). *Statistical significance at the 5% level.

Fig. 2   Shareholders' abnormal return at deal announcement.

Researchers	Years	Obs. (A/T)	Acquirers 3-day CAR	Targets 3-day CAR
Pettway and Yamada (1986)	1977–1984	50/16	0.82% (N)	0.07% (N)
Kang, Shivdasani and Yamada (2000)	1977–1993	154/N	0.90% (S)	N.A.
Inoue (2002)	1990–1998	49/48	−1.19% (I)	1.08% (I)
	1999–2002	89/100	3.01% (S)	5.96% (S)
	1990–2002	138/148	1.51% (S)	4.37% (S)
This research	2003–2007	379/382	1.16% (S)	8.18% (S)

A: Acquirers, T: Targets, S: Statistically significant at 10% level, I: Statistically insignificant, N: N.A.

Fig. 3   Summary of shareholders' return from M&As in Japan.

target firms, it is positive (about 2% both in Japan and in the United States). These results imply that, on an average, M&As in Japan increase shareholder value and M&As support the economic rationale as is the case for those in the United States. Moreover, since M&As should be strongly supported by shareholders of target firms and there should be no strong opposition from the shareholders of acquirer firms, shareholders in general should support M&As. In sum, an active M&A market leads to efficiency gain for the companies and wealth maximization of shareholders. Figure 3 shows the empirical results of shareholders' return at the announcement of M&As in Japan. The results reported by other researchers are largely consistent with the aforementioned results.

Although M&As increase shareholder value in Japan, it also turns out that the main winners in M&As are the shareholders of the target firms. This result is similar to the empirical results reported by Jensen and Ruback (1983), which surveyed the empirical results of M&As from 1950s to 1980s in the United States. The distribution of the wealth among the shareholders is interpreted as an evidence that potential acquirers compete with each other to acquire the control of the target firm, and that an acquirer who can bid the highest price for the target firm gains the control. In such a competitive market, the control of a target firm is expected to be taken over by a management team who can maximize the value of a target firm.

In Japan, such wealth distribution between acquirer and target shareholders emerged only after the late 1990s when an M&A boom began and a market mechanism began to work. However, in Japan, the shareholders of acquirer firms still gain a part of the wealth creation from M&As, which is not the case in the United States. This difference might be caused by different levels of acquisition premiums in the two countries. In the United States, between 1970s and 1990s, the acquisition premium (premium of takeover price over stock price just before the initial announcement of deals) has been approximately 40% on an average and in Japan, between 2000 and 2007, it has been 7% on an average. This difference directly influences the distribution of wealth between acquirer and target shareholders.

In fact, the M&A market in the United States is a very active and competitive market. According to Andrade *et al.* (2001), in 4000 M&A deals between the 1970s and 1990s, the average number of potential acquirers was 1.4 per target firm. Such a competitive M&A market resulted in a much larger acquisition premium than was the case in the market with less competition. In the competitive market, even in cases without actual competition, a large acquisition premium is paid to prevent potential competition. Consequently, in the United States, an acquisition premium as large as 40% has prevailed. Thus, in a competitive market, the return on acquirers' shareholders breaks even or is even negative.

In comparison with the US market, the Japanese M&A market is considerably less competitive. There was no case wherein two or more acquirers compete with each other to acquire the same public firm until the 1990s. Although a competitive bid for the same public firms was conducted in this decade, they are still exceptional cases. Consequently, it seems that the acquirers in Japan have also obtained a part of the wealth from announced M&As, owing to the lower acquisition premium. Even in the 2000s, when M&A activities in Japan increased and the acquisition premiums become larger than those in the previous decades, the shareholders of acquirer firms are still enjoying a positive return. Such evidence can be interpreted to mean that the Japanese M&A market is currently not as competitive as that in the United States. However, we can predict that the managers of Japanese firms increasingly seek M&A opportunities, since they do increase the shareholder value. This, in turn, would render the Japanese M&A market more competitive and efficient.

4 Factors Behind the Value Creation by M&A Activities

In the previous section, I showed that M&A activities in Japan contribute to an increase in shareholder value of both acquirer and target firms. What factors are responsible for value creation?

Inoue and Kato (2003) analyzed the factors behind CAR of acquirer and target firms on the basis of certain major hypotheses regarding the creation and destruction of shareholder value via M&As considering characteristics of Japanese M&As. The classification by major characteristics of M&A deals among public firms in Japan from 1990 to 2002 are shown in Fig. 4.

Figure 4 shows that one fourth of the sample aims to rescue the troubled target firms. Moreover, 45% of the deals are conducted between affiliated (capital-related) firms; a half of the rescue deals, in particular, occur between affiliated firms. This is consistent with the aforementioned view that the Japanese M&A market is less competitive than that in the United States.

Kester (1991), who investigated M&A activities in Japan in the late 1980s, advocated that economic benefit resulting from a disciplinary role of the market for corporate control was not important in Japan wherein the monitoring system based on timely interventions

Deal purpose	Relationship	N	Horizontal deal	Acquisition premium
Non-rescue	Affiliated	46 (32%)	17 (37%)	8.8% (3.10)
	Non-affiliated	61 (42%)	56 (92%)	7.1% (2.80)
	Sub-total	107 (74%)	73 (68%)	7.9% (4.16)
Rescue	Affiliated	18 (13%)	8 (44%)	3.9% (0.77)
	Non-affiliated	19 (13%)	18 (95%)	−10.4% (−1.60)
	Sub-total	37 (26%)	26 (70%)	−3.3% (−0.77)
Total		144 (100%)	99 (69%)	5.1% (2.80)

Relationship: if an acquirer holds more than 20% equity ownership of the target, the deal is classified in an affiliated deal, otherwise the deal is classified as a non-affiliated deal. Horizontal: if an acquirer and the target are in the same industry, defined by Tokyo Stock Exchange Code, the deal is categorized in a horizontal deal. Acquisition premium: % difference between acquisition price and stock price of target of one day before the acquisition price announcement. Inside of a parenthesis shows (1) N: % in the total sample, (2) Horizontal Deal: % in each sub-sample, (3) Acquisition premium: t-stat.

Fig. 4   Deal characteristics of M&As in Japan.

by affiliated firms and main banks developed and prevailed. The assertion by Kester regarding the Japanese M&A market still seems to be quite applicable to the period analyzed herein.

Figure 4 also shows that 69% of the entire sample and 93% of non-affiliated deals are horizontal deals within the same industry. Furthermore, from our analysis of the detailed contents of business, we find that in most of the deals that were not classified as horizontal, close business relationships including vertical ones exist between acquirer and target firms. Therefore, most of the deals between public firms in Japan aim to achieve synergistic gain from the integration of the same line of business and there are few conglomerates and pure financial deals. Such a high rate of horizontal deals is an important characteristic of the M&As between Japanese firms. In the United States, horizontal deals constituted only 42% of the deals from 1973 to 1998 as reported by Andrade et al. (2001).

To examine if the aforementioned characteristics of M&As in Japan influence shareholders' return of acquirer and target firms, we investigate the CAR of sub-sample divided by if a deal was a rescue or non-rescue deal and a horizontal or diversification deal. The result is shown in Fig. 5.

Purpose	Horizontal deal	N	Acquirer 3-day CAR	Target 3-days CAR	Acquisition premium
Non-rescue	Non-horizontal	34	0.8% (0.59)	4.6%** (2.06)	11.1%*** (3.62)
	Horizontal	73	3.1%** (2.43)	5.8%*** (3.58)	6.3%*** (2.68)
	Difference		−2.3% (−1.08)	−1.2% (−0.41)	4.8% (1.19)
Rescue	Non-horizontal	11	−4.0% (−1.75)	−2.3% (−0.56)	3.8% (0.52)
	Horizontal	26	−0.6% (−0.37)	1.3% (0.41)	−6.4% (−1.24)
	Difference		−3.4% (−1.14)	−3.6% (−0.64)	10.2% (1.12)

Horizontal: if an acquirer and the target are in the same industry, defined by Tokyo Stock Exchange Code, the deal is categorized in a horizontal, otherwise categorized in a non-horizontal. Acquisition premium: % difference between acquisition price and stock price of target of one day before the acquisition price announcement. Inside of a parenthesis shows t–statistics. *, **, ***Statistical significance at the 10%, 5%, and 1% levels, respectively, for two-tailed tests.

Fig. 5   Deal characteristics and shareholders' abnormal return.

Figure 5 shows that the positive and significant abnormal returns for shareholders are observed only with the non-rescue and horizontal deals for both acquirer and target firms. These results indicate that expected synergistic gain arising from the M&As between two firms in the same industry constitutes the dominant cause behind the positive abnormal return for shareholders in Japan.

Figure 5 also shows that there is a difference in the acquisition premium between rescue and non-rescue deals. The difference is significant at a 1% level with the two-tailed test. In a deal wherein large value creation is expected, the management of the acquirer firm rationally recognizes economical room for the payment of a large premium. However, Bradley, Desai and Kim (1988), and Sirower (1997) showed that there was a negative relation between the size of the acquisition premium and shareholder return for acquirer firms in the United States. Such a negative relation supports the wealth transfer hypothesis that the oversized acquisition premium merely transfers wealth from shareholders of acquirer firms to those of target firms. This trend is consistent with the hubris hypothesis that Roll (1986) posited.

To examine if acquisition premium in Japan represents a reasonable estimate of value creation from M&As or management hubris,

Dependent variable	Acquirer 3-day CAR	Target 3-day CAR
N	113	113
Adj. R^2	0.08	0.16
Coefficient	0.01	−0.01
	(0.28)	(−0.18)
Acquisition premium	−0.14***	0.24***
	(−2.62)	(2.97)
Acquisition premium *Rescue dummy	0.19**	0.11
	(2.26)	(0.94)
Rescue dummy	−0.05***	−0.04
(Rescue deal = 1, Others = 0)	(−2.84)	(−1.30)
Horizontal dummy	0.03	0.05
(Horizontal deal = 1, Others = 0)	(1.62)	(1.49)
Affiliated dummy	0.02	0.03
(Affiliated deal = 1, Others = 0)	(0.91)	(1.00)
Deal cancel dummy	−0.03	0.01
(Canceled deal = 1, Completed deal = 0)	(−0.80)	(0.09)

Acquisition premium: % difference between acquisition price and stock price of target of one day before the acquisition price announcement. Horizontal: if an acquirer and the target are in the same industry, defined by Tokyo Stock Exchange Code, the deal is categorized in a horizontal deal. Affiliated deal: if an acquirer holds more than 20% equity ownership of the target, the deal is classified in an affiliated deal. Deal cancel: if an announced deal is cancelled later, the deal is categorized in a canceled deal, otherwise it is categorized in a completed deal. Inside of a parenthesis shows t-statistics. *,**,*** Statistical significance at the 10%, 5%, and 1% levels, respectively.

Fig. 6   Factors behind shareholders' abnormal return.

Inoue and Kato (2003) conducted multiple regression analysis. Figure 6 shows the results.

Figure 6 shows that the acquisition premium and rescue dummy variable respectively have a significant negative effect on shareholder return of acquirer firms. First, the result confirms that rescue deals do not contribute to the shareholder value of acquirers. Second, the result is consistent with the wealth transfer (hubris) hypothesis that observed acquisition premiums in non-rescue deals does represent the wealth distribution between acquirer and target shareholders to some extent. However, since the shareholder return for acquirer firms is positive on an average, the level of management hubris should be less serious in Japan than in the United States.

The distinction between affiliated and non-affiliated deals and horizontal and diversifying deals do not have any significant effect on the shareholders' return of acquirer firms. However, t-statistics for the positive coefficient of the horizontal deal dummy is as high as 1.62 which is close to the significance level at 10%. This constitutes weak evidence wherein the major factor for value creation from M&As is a synergistic gain from the integration of the same line of business. On the other hand, as for shareholder return of target firms, only the acquisition premium showed positive effect which is statistically significant at 1% level. Therefore, the shareholder return of the target firm is not related to any analyzed deal characteristics but it depends solely on the acquisition premium offered by acquirer firms.

As for the method of payment for the acquisitions, cash constitutes 15% of the sample and stock constitutes 85%. Even when the dummy variable for cash payment is added to the regression model, above result does not change. Moreover, the payment method, cash or stock, does not have a significant impact on the shareholders' return. Hanamura, Inoue, and Suzuki (2009) analyze the differences between cash and stock deals with a larger sample, which consist of deals from 2000 to 2008, and they find that cash deals show a significantly higher shareholders' return than stock deals for target firms; however, there is no significant difference in shareholders' return between cash deals and stock deals for acquirer firms. This result is inconsistent with results reported in the United States wherein shareholders' return for acquirers in stock deals is significantly lower than that in cash deals.

5   Long-Term Shareholders' Return after M&As in Japan

The aforementioned analysis of shareholders' return at the initial announcement of the deals is based on the assumption that the stock market is efficient. If the market is completely efficient, since the expected economic effect of an M&A deal is fully reflected in stock prices of both acquirer and target firms in the short-period, an abnormal return should not be found in the long-term stock price. However, in the United States, shareholders' long-term return of acquirer firms (three years to five years) after the announcement of the deals is reported to be negative (Agrawal, Jaffe, and Mandelker, 1992; Rau and Vermaelen, 1998). This can be seen as a form of counterevidence to the efficient market hypothesis. On the other hand, Fama (1998) has pointed out that unlike the analysis of shareholders' return in the short-time window, a bias will arise from the selection of the analytical model or the benchmark in the analysis of long-term abnormal return. Andrade *et al.* (2001) insisted that the shareholder's return after the announcement is an appropriate indicator for the evaluation of the influence of an M&A on shareholder value, since it cannot be said that the significant long-term abnormal return for acquirer firms exists from their own long-term return analysis, and since a theory that predicts a long-term abnormal return is also absent.

Inoue and Kato (2004) show long-term shareholders' return after M&As for the first time in Japan. Although we recognized that an analytical model and benchmark selection would have significant influence on the result of long-term shareholders' return analysis, there was only limited number of samples that enable us to analyze long-term shareholders' return after M&A at the point and we could not perform a detailed robustness test. Therefore, the analysis is limited for highlighting the trend of long-term shareholders' return on the basis of the traditional method with which to test the abnormal return from the market model.

We analyzed shareholders' return for the three years after an M&A by considering the CAR and buy-and-hold abnormal return (BHAR). With regard to the sample, in order to limit it to economically material deals for acquirer firms, we selected deals wherein the market capitalization or the book value of total assets of target firm exceeded 20% of that of the acquirer firm from the same samples which we analyzed the shareholders' return at the announcement in the previous sections. The result is shown in Fig. 7.

With regard to CAR, the abnormal return for three years after the initial announcement of the deals is positive and significant at the 5% level in both market adjustment and market model. In order to confirm that the observed positive abnormal return is caused by the M&A, we compared three-year CAR before and after the deal announcement. We used the CAR obtained by the market

		CAR			BHAR
		Market adjusted		Market model	Market model
		3 years before announcement	3 years after announcement	3 years after announcement	3 year after announcement
All sample	N	73	73	73	73
	Mean	−3.3%	15.9%**	21.8%**	2.6%
	t-stat	−0.491	2.353	2.317	0.292
Sub-sample by payment method					
Stock	N	67	67	67	67
	Mean	−9.5%	17.2%**	26.9%***	9.1%
	t-stat	−1.641	2.381	2.805	1.190
Cash	N	6	6	6	6
	Mean	66.5%	1.0%	−34.8%	−70.1%
	t-stat	1.623	0.064	−0.973	−1.146

**, ***Statistical significance at the 5% and 1% levels, respectively.

Fig. 7   Long-term abnormal return after a deal announcement.

adjustment model wherein the parameter estimation from the prior period is unnecessary. From the analysis, we confirmed that the three years of abnormal return after the announcement is higher than that before the announcement and the difference is statistically significant at the 5% level. Thus, it can be said that the shareholders' return for an acquiring firm has improved with the M&A.

On the other hand, from BHAR analysis, the abnormal return for the three years is also positive, but it is not statistically significant. Thus, the robustness of the results wherein the long-term abnormal return of an acquiring firm is positive is questionable and, at this point, it requires future research with a larger sample base.

Since there is no evidence that shareholder value decreases in the long term after the deal announcement, the conclusion we derived from the analysis presented in the previous sections that M&A increases shareholders' value should hold.

6   Conclusion

This paper summarizes the changes and the characteristics of the Japanese M&A market and also showed that M&As between Japanese firms increase shareholder value. The synergistic gain from the combination of the two firms in the same industry is the major reason behind value creation.

This paper insists that the Japanese M&A market has not yet developed into a fully competitive market as in the United States and it also insists that the overpayment in M&A has not posed a serious problem for acquirer firms in Japan, which has not been the case in the United States. Thus, there is a trade-off, but the former can be seen as a source of inefficiency of the Japanese M&A market in the sense that a proposed deal is not necessarily the most efficient combination of firms in the market.

However, the Japanese M&A market is changing such that its market mechanism will work more efficiently. As for hostile takeovers and competitive bids, although there are no incidences between listed companies in the sample from 1990 to 2002, there were several trials in the period 2003 and 2007. Although almost all attempts at hostile takeovers are unsuccessful, the management of Japanese firms presently acknowledge that they can be successful. In recent years, there are two incidences wherein friendly mergers between listed Japanese firms were rejected by shareholders of the respective target firms due to insufficient acquisition premium. Reflecting increasing pressure from shareholders, acquisition premium is increasing.

Furthermore, activist hedge funds are increasing their presence after 2000. Inoue and Kato (2007) analyzed block-share purchase by activist hedge funds more than one-hundred Japanese firms from 2000 to 2005 and they found that these funds were targeting inefficiently managed value-firms and they contributed to increase the shareholder value of the target firms in the long run. This indicates that the Japanese M&A market has performed a disciplinary function for management, as was the case in the United States and Britain.

Until the mid-1990s, the role of the M&A market was considered to be limited in Japan, as the corporate culture in Japan is so different from those in the United States and Britain. However, as this paper shows, the Japanese M&A market has come to resemble that in the United States over the last ten years. That is, the Japanese M&A market is no longer unique. In the deregulated market in Japan, M&As are expected to serve as an essential and effective form of competitive strategy for firms and they serve as an important mechanism which help to discipline inefficient management.

Acknowledgment

This study has been funded by a National Kagaku-Kenkyuhi fellowship.

References

Agrawal, A, JF Jaffe and GM Mandelker (1992). The post merger performance of acquiring firms: Re-examination of an anomaly. *Journal of Finance*, 47(4), 1605–1671.

Andrade, G, M Mitchell and E Stafford (2001). New evidence and perspectives on mergers. *Journal of Economic Perspectives*, 15(2), 103–120.

Bradley, M, A Desai and EH Kim (1988). Synergistic gain from corporate acquisitions and their divisions between the stockholders of target and acquiring firms. *Journal of Financial Economics*, 21(1), 3–40.

Coase, RH (1937). The nature of the firm. *Economica*, 4, 386–405.

Fama, EF (1998). Market efficiency, long-term returns, and behavioral finance. *Journal of Financial Economics*, 49(3), 283–306.

Hanamura, S, K Inoue and K Suzuki (2009). Bidder and target valuation and method of payment of M&As in Japan: Evidence against the misvaluation driven takeovers, Working Paper.

Inoue, K (2002). Analysis of stock price reaction to the M&A announcements in Japan focusing on the type of transactions. *Japan Journal of Finance*, 22(2), 107–120 (in Japanese).

Inoue, K (2008). Protection of minority shareholders' interests in M&A. *Syouken Keizai Gakkai Nenpou*, 43, 212–216 (in Japanese).

Inoue, K and HK Kato (2003). An empirical analysis of factors of shareholders' abnormal return at M&A announcement. *Gendai Finance*, 13, 3–28 (in Japanese).

Inoue, K and HK Kato (2004). Do corporate acquisitions increase shareholder wealth? Evidence from the U.S. and Japan. *Securities Analyst Journal*, 42(10), 33–43 (in Japanese).

Inoue, K and HK Kato (2006). *M&A and Stock Market*, Toyo-Keizai-Sinposha (in Japanese).

Inoue, K and HK Kato (2007). An evaluation of activist funds in Japan. *The Economic Review*, 58(3), 203–216 (in Japanese).

Jensen, MC and RS Ruback (1983). The market for corporate control: The scientific evidence. *Journal of Financial Economics*, 11(1), 5–50.

Kang, J, A Shivdasani and T Yamada (2000). The effect of bank relations on investment decisions: An investigation of Japanese takeover bids. *Journal of Finance*, 55(5), 2197–2218.

Kester, WC (1991). *Japanese Takeovers*. Harvard Business School Press.

Mitchell, ML and JH Mulherin (1996). The impact of industry shocks on takeover and restructuring activity. *Journal of Financial Economics*, 41(2), 193–229.

Pettway, RH and T Yamada (1986). Mergers in Japan and their impacts upon stockholders' wealth. *Financial Management*, 15(Winter), 43–52.

Rau, PR and T Vermaelen (1998). Glamour, value, and the post-acquisition performance of acquiring firms. *Journal of Financial Economics*, 49(2), 223–253.

Roll, R (1986). The hubris theory of corporate takeovers. *Journal of Business*, 59(2), 197–216.

Sirower, ML (1997). *The Synergy Trap: How Companies Lose the Acquisition Game*. The Free Press.

Index